52 wisdom tales

from around the world

DOORWAYS TO THE

SOUL

EDITED BY

ELISA DAVY PEARMAIN

～ ～ ～

RESOURCE *Publications* · Eugene, Oregon

Thanks to:

Ron O'Reilly, who helped me to see that this is
a well-worn path.

Vicki, Carla, and Lennie, who first let me say the
word *God*.

Doug Lipman, who introduced me to wisdom stories.

My husband, daughter, mother, father,
and brother, and Diane and all of my friends for
your love and support.

Special thanks to Margaret Carpenter for her generous
editing expertise and insights, and to Peter Thomson
for his invaluable help with the computer.

Biblical quotations are from the New Revised Standard Version of the Bible, © 1989 by
the Division of Christian Education of the National Council of the Churches of Christ in
the U.S.A., and are used by permission

Resource Publications
A division of Wipf and Stock Publishers
199 W 8th Ave, Suite 3
Eugene, OR 97401

Doorways to the Soul
52 Wisdom Tales from Around the World
Edited by Pearmain, Elisa Davy
Copyright©1998 The Pilgrim Press
ISBN 13: 978-1-55635-740-4
ISBN 10: 1-55635-740-0
Publication date 11/30/2007
Previously published by The Pilgrim Press, 1998

CONTENTS

❦

INTRODUCTION

STORIES AND SPIRITUALITY

ONCE UPON A TIME when the earth was new, the Creator decided that she wanted to play a game of hide-and-go-seek . . .

It was at about this same time that the Creator's angels were having a meeting. They were afraid that people might try to kidnap or monopolize God, and so they decided that she had to be hidden in a safe place, a place where all people would be able to find her if they searched, but where none could own her exclusively. So they sent out angel scouts to find this perfect place . . .

Meanwhile the Creator had already found her hiding place, the safest, fairest and warmest place to hide, and yet the most difficult to find: inside each and every human heart.[1]

There is a story told of the Hasidic master Rabbi Barukh and a time when his grandson Yeheil was playing hide-and-go-seek with a friend. Yeheil hid himself well and waited a long time for his friend to find him. Finally he came out of his hiding place only to discover that his friend had not been looking for him at all. Discovering this, Yeheil ran to his grandfather in tears at his friend's faithlessness. Then tears brimmed in Rabbi Barukh's eyes, and he said: "God says the same thing: 'I hide, but no one wants to seek me.' "[2]

Yet each in our own way, we are looking, or at least longing, for an experience of being truly alive and touching God, or what is "God-like" in ourselves and in each other. We all have experienced the grace and wisdom of God or the highest truth at various times in our lives. When we treasure these experiences as stories, and retell them to ourselves and others, we are drawn closer to them. When we hear the stories of others we are similarly reminded of our own knowing.

The journey toward God or truth or wholeness is not an easy one. Entering into our own hearts is a quest often fraught with fear, pain, and the frustrations of a vigilant ego; but it is a well-worn path. We can find great comfort, joy, and humor in the stories of those who have stumbled or danced down the path before us.

Talking about things spiritual is something most of us do only with trusted friends or relations. It is so personal, this relationship we have and the beliefs we struggle with and hold dear. It is so common to feel afraid that we will be called crazy, or said to have gone off the deep end, if we try to express our honest longings or deepest beliefs. And yet we need to share these with others to satisfy our longing for connection, and to validate our feelings and desires. Stories are a wonderful conduit into the discussion of things spiritual. We open ourselves up to stories and experience them with body, mind, and spirit. Stories are safe in that they are about people other than ourselves, inhabiting other times and places.

Spirituality is very personal, and I do not take lightly the task of speaking of it. This book is meant to be ecumenical, seeking to connect people from all faiths through story. Not only do we come from different cultural and religious backgrounds, but we come to the spiritual journey for different reasons. For many of us the spiritual journey is the desire for connection, connection to a God, or to what is the highest truth, or sacred. We seek connection to the deepest part of ourselves where that truth resides. We seek connection to one another. We seek to remember our connection to the earth our mother, and all of her creatures, our brothers and sisters. Many of us embark on a spiritual journey to make meaning of our experiences. Quite often we enter into a spiritual journey as a lifesaving part of the healing or recovery process. And for many of us it is the desire to live better, to transcend the day-to-day suffering and keep our eye on the big picture, as the Zen master in this story demonstrates:

DURING A TIME of civil war in Korea, a general led his troops through province after province, overrunning whatever stood in his path. The people of one town, knowing that he was coming and having heard tales of his cruelty, all fled into the mountains. The general arrived with his troops and sent them out to search the empty town. Some of the soldiers came back and reported that only one person remained, a Zen priest. The general strode over to the temple, walked in, pulled out his sword, and said, "Don't you know who I am? I am the one who can run through you without batting an eye."

The Zen priest looked back at him calmly and responded, "And I, sir, am one who can be run through without batting an eye." The general, hearing this, bowed and left.[3]

The spiritual journey is the process of learning to know oneself and becoming self-aware. We learn to love ourselves as the sacred beings that we are, and discover in that love that we are connected to all that exists; thus we develop compassion and strength. The journey is a process of letting go of old interpretations of self and of others that no longer serve us, to make room for the new. What would you add to this definition of the spiritual journey?

Passing wisdom on through stories is a tradition as old as language itself. Great spiritual masters from every culture and time have relied on stories to do their teaching. Common folks have also used story as a way of passing on wisdom, and these folktales and biographical stories are equally valuable sources of inspiration and learning.

Some wisdom stories are told in a simple, straightforward manner. Others speak in metaphor or are shrouded in symbolism. Some stories seek to shake us out of a logical way of thinking so that we might be opened to new understandings. Stories have many layers of meaning. We will take from them what we need and what we are ready for at the time.

But why does wisdom come so often in the form of stories?

The author Anthony de Mello tells of a master who always gave his teachings in parables and stories, much to the frustration of his disciples, who longed for something more to ease their understanding. To their objections the master would answer, "You have yet to understand, my dears, that the shortest distance between truth and a human being is a story."[4]

One reason that the disciples were frustrated with the stories of the master was probably that the disciples had to decipher their meanings themselves. But as one master put it, "How would you like to have someone offer you fruit and then chew it for you?"[5] The process of making meaning is very personal.

Why are stories such a powerful medium? Let me offer some of the reasons that I know: Stories speak to us through images, pictures, and symbols. This is the language of the imagination. Images endure in our minds and our hearts long after the words are gone. Research bears out that lessons and facts are remembered better when taught through story.[6]

We relate to story in part because its basic, almost universal structure mirrors our experience of being human: facing conflicts, garnering inner and outer resources, and transforming. We are naturally interested in the stories of how others transform, because they provide clues for our own life journeys.

There is magic in stories, and young and old crave them. The words "Once upon a time . . ." or even the word "Once . . ." immediately suspends ordinary reality, relaxing and transporting us.

Clarissa Pinkola Estés, a renowned storyteller, author, and psychotherapist, refers to stories as "medicine," likening the energy released in stories to the action of an antibiotic. She says: "Story travels to the place in the psyche where it is most needed. Story can be used as a medicine that once transmitted, can remain and act within the psyche . . . long after the last word has been spoken."[7]

Stories are not just for children. Only in the last few hundred years among industrialized cultures have fairy tales and folktales been relegated to the exclusive domain of children. Only in the last fifty years or less have families significantly decreased the amount of time they spend sharing family stories intergenerationally.

Stories also speak to us through feelings, the language of our hearts. As we experience vicariously the feelings of another, we open those protected places in ourselves and find the courage to visit our own emotions and memories.

Stories connect us to people too. When we walk in the shoes of others through story we learn to empathize with their experience, and they are no longer strangers to us. The commonality of our stories can bind us across cultures and time. Perhaps our modern world-myth is to realize our connection to not just one family or one race but to all the peoples of the human race.

The fact that we can experience the stories of others vicariously has great significance; their stories become our stories, and once we have visited them, we can revisit, trying the experience on again and again, until we experience transformation.

A Swahili folk tale that I love reminds us so well that stories are soul food:

THERE ONCE LIVED a sultan who had riches beyond compare. One day his wife began to grow thin and weak. No matter what foods he had prepared for her she continued to deteriorate. One day the sultan noticed that one of his servants, a poor man, had a wife who was plump and full of life and vigor. The sultan asked the poor man what he fed his wife. "It is simple," the man replied. "I feed her meat of the tongue." The sultan then ordered his chefs to prepare tongues from every possible beast and fowl, but still his wife withered away.

Finally in desperation the sultan demanded that the poor man's wife exchange places with his wife so that she might be restored to good health. Immediately the sultan's wife began to thrive and the poor man's to wither and fade. The sultan admired his wife and asked her, "What is it that he fed you, wife? I must know." "My husband," she answered, "the meat of the tongue that your servant fed me wasn't the tongue of an animal, but stories, poetry, and songs that roll off of the tongue and fill the heart full. This is what makes a woman thrive."[8]

I have collected stories from many spiritual and cultural traditions. Although their form may reflect the cultural and religious idiosyncrasies of their time and place, their messages are remarkably universal. In my research I repeatedly encountered in every culture the same principles basic to spiritual development: Do no harm, practice generosity and loving-kindness, know thyself and follow your highest thought, be aware of the effects of your actions, practice gratitude and forgiveness, enter into direct relationship with the source of life through prayer or meditation (silence). I have chosen stories to which my heart responded with a resounding "Aha!", stories that speak to these principles and other aspects of being a human being on a spiritual journey.

I have tried to balance the male/female imagery associated with the Creator, as well as to acknowledge that for many of us God is not a person, but an energy or creative force. I do not wish to impose my beliefs on you but hope to make the stories available to you as a gift so that you will take what you need and pass it on.

These are short stories that can be easily read, remembered, and shared with others. You will find them handy in all sorts of situations. They are short enough that you can keep them in your memory's pocket and whip them out to make a point in any situation, with adults or children.

Although I envision adults as my primary readers, families may find that sharing these stories creates wonderful opportunities for developing imagery and vicarious experience, as well as providing alternative solutions to challenging problems they face. "Hey, Dad, remember that story about the king who felt angry?"

Why did I choose to collect spiritual and wisdom stories? Like many of you, I have considered the development of my connection to the Creator and the resulting flow of love and compassion to be my life's most important goal. But I find little support in the outer world to guide or sustain this focus. As a storyteller and therapist, I know that to hear and tell stories, both personal and traditional, brings profound healing and nourishment. To search out and live with these wisdom tales helped me remember my experiences of God's grace and stay closer to the longing and the mystery present in daily life. When I take the time to read and ponder these stories I am inevitably reminded that God is an active player in this game of hide-and-seek, perhaps a lot like the small child who cannot wait to be found and so calls out, "Here I am, here I am!"

SUGGESTIONS FOR USING THIS BOOK

Stories are doorways into seeing and experiencing your inner and outer worlds. After reading a story you can explore this new terrain over and over by reentering the doorway.

These stories are intended to be taken in small doses. When we read more than a few at one sitting, we stop pondering and begin consuming. It is as if we read a sign on the stories' door that tells about the story, but we do not open the door to be touched by the story. I hope you can see that the door opens inward!

When I was first introduced to stories I would read through collection after collection at a rapid pace, waiting for the "perfect" stories to grab me. Occasionally something would jump out at me, but many other valuable stories passed me by because I had not taken more time with them. Stories need time to sink in so that their images may connect with our hearts and imaginations, and personal meaning and learning may arise.

I have organized this book so that you will read one story per week. You may prefer to read through the whole collection first and then try my approach later. If you wish to read more, then of course read the stories at your own pace. I suggest that you get some bookmarks to mark the ones that especially appeal to you, and on the top of the bookmark write an identifying word to help you remember what you liked. You can then return to the stories later to contemplate them by theme.

Some of the stories will be familiar to you. A first reaction might be to say, "Oh, I already know this one" and to skip over it, as we might a favorite TV show that is a rerun. But what does it mean to "know" a story? In earlier times, when stories were passed on by oral means, stories were heard over and over hundreds of times to assure that the listeners knew them. Rather than skipping over stories that are familiar, I urge you to take your knowing to a deeper level.

I have not categorized the stories by theme, but have chosen to mix themes so that you encounter different types of dilemmas each week. I have also interspersed the cultures of origin, and alternated humor with the more serious parables.

Just as hearing and contemplating a sermon once a week is a ritual for many people, reading and working with the stories can become so also. Rituals are helpful in ordering our lives. Rituals give a feeling of saneness and meaningfulness. I suggest therefore that you ritualize your reading of these tales in the ways that work best for you. You might read one aloud at the dinner table at the start of the new week or before bedtime. Making a ritual of reading the stories will heighten your experience.

I also suggest that you work and live with the ideas in a story in order to discover and deepen its personal significance to you. I have included a few questions following each story to help you make a personal connection with the story. Sometimes questions, like keys, can give us a needed angle which opens the story door inward. Each of us will find our own meaning to the story, for stories are usually multilayered. Please do not let my questions or comments supersede or negate your own interpretations. If this happens, wait to read my follow-up ideas when you have thoroughly explored and honored your own.

Working with the Stories

Having a week's time to think about only one story will allow you to mull it over in your mind. Mulling over a story greatly deepens its helpfulness to you. It becomes your story, a part of your language and culture, a blueprint that you can superimpose onto your own life. Stories, like dreams, help you whether you pay extra attention to them or not. They are calming and healing. When you do decide to pay attention to stories, as when you pay attention to dreams, you often understand the personal significance of the symbolism and imagery, and then these images become touchstones for your daily life.

Some ways to mull over the stories consciously are as follows:

1. Go for a walk in a quiet place and contemplate a story and how to apply its wisdom to your life.
2. Contemplate a story while sitting in meditation.
3. Ask the story characters to share their wisdom with you in writing. Using the "free-writing" style described below, simply ask the characters a question and then write from your own mind an unedited answer.
4. Ask the story or its characters to share their wisdom through your dreams. Before falling asleep at night, think about the story and ask your subconscious mind for a dream. First thing in the morning, write down your dreams. If you pay little attention to your dreams, they may not rise to conscious memory or be clear to you. If, however, you take the time to remember, record, and consider them, your dreams will become clearer and more obviously relevant.
5. Mull over the story out loud with others. Read the stories aloud with someone else and share your reactions and what the story means to you. When has the experience recounted in the story happened or not happened to you? What would it mean for you

to respond as the story character did? How could you apply this
to your life?

After each story there is a sequence of follow-up suggestions. The follow-up suggestions are explained below.

Exploring the Story. I like to start by exploring the story terrain.
This has two dimensions: We enter into the world of the story, which
stands on its own, apart from us, with its own structure and cultural context. At the same time we explore where the story lives in our imagination, and what meaning it holds in our hearts, bodies, and minds.

Exploring the story apart from how it lives in us involves exploring
what you know and researching what you don't know about the story's
culture of origin. This can entail finding books to give you a picture of
the land and its people, and talking with people who come from the culture about the cultural and historical context of the stories.

Visualizing the Story. To find where the story lives in you, explore
the story imagery, its characters, dilemmas, and themes. This is done by
engaging your imagination so that the images go to where they are needed.
Our brains process information and store memories in very complicated
ways, ways that involve the senses and emotions. Processing information
is about making connections between old information and new. You can
enhance this process on a conscious and unconscious level by exploring
the story imagery.

I invite the reader to engage the imagination by visualizing the story
using all of the senses. Close your eyes and go in your imagination to the
setting where the story takes place. You may feel more comfortable imagining that you are watching a movie, but I suggest getting even more
active. Really walk around in that setting; see, smell, touch, taste, hear
and feel emotions as you watch the story unfold. Once your imagery is
attached to the story, the story sometimes takes on a whole new meaning.

Writing about the Story. Next, write about the story in order to
work with its ideas and cultural context. Consider questions such as:
What do I think this story meant to the original teller? What did I like

about the story? What doesn't make sense to me about the story? What reminded me of own life? What bothered me? How could I try to apply the story's lesson to my own life? Try using a "free-writing" style in which you write for a certain length of time without stopping (literally) or editing, and in which you make no effort to push aside painful feelings or thoughts.

Exploring the Story through an Expressive Art Form. Perhaps you like to write poetry, to paint, or to construct three-dimensional representations. Perhaps you sing, or do interpretive dance, or create improvisational pieces of music. Play with the ideas in the story and retell it through your chosen art form. Bring the story to life in a way that has meaning for you. According to the author and psychologist Howard Gardner, there are (at least) seven different styles that we humans use to learn and process information—logical/mathematical, visual/spatial, musical, linguistic, kinesthetic, interpersonal, and intrapersonal.[9] Some of us, for example, are more comfortable working with information that comes to us visually; others need a kinesthetic experience. By exploring story through an expressive art form that you enjoy (and you don't have to be an expert at it), you allow for new ways of learning. If we employ only the intellect, we may miss the surest path to direct experience. Direct experience opens us to ecstasy. An ecstatic experience is one in which we feel totally connected to what we are doing, and as a result, connected to the whole universe, or that which feels like spirit to us. Expressing our own creativity from a deep place of truth is a truly satisfying, deeply joyous experience.

Because this is a book on storytelling, I will suggest a method of exploring through story making. I call this "waking dreaming," a Jungian term for using dream images or other symbols that stand out for a person while awake to learn about the subconscious. To create a waking dream, select some of the symbols or images from the story that stand out for you, things like keys, doorways, seeds, deserts, and let a spontaneous story weave out from your imagination. See where it takes you without trying to control it. This works best when telling the story to someone as it unfolds or into a tape recorder. It works especially well when the teller has his or her eyes closed.

Making a Personal Connection with the Story. In order to make a personal connection to the story you must do some autobiographical searching. Recollect times in your life when you grappled (or refused to grapple) with the same issues presented in the story. Sometimes this involves writing a brainstorm list of memories on a certain theme. Starting with your earliest memories and using places and people as touchstones, write a word or two to describe the memory, then move on. If, for example, the theme is prayer, you might start with your earliest memories and write a list of things people told you about prayer, favorite childhood prayers, stories you remember hearing in a religious context, experiences in which you prayed for something you did or didn't want. For example:

I REMEMBER HAVING one of many fights with my parents one evening as a pre-teen. They left shortly after the argument and went to a party. My grandmother was staying with us at the time because my grandfather had recently died. She scolded me that I shouldn't fight with my parents because they could die just like he did. I felt so guilty and terrified that I wrote a letter to God praying that he would bring them home safely. I put the note outside on my windowsill just to be sure it was received. Even into my late twenties I kept a windowsill shrine for God in my bedroom, associating God as out in nature rather than within and ever-present.

Memories beget memories, so even those of us with not so good memories begin remembering when we use this process. Another approach is to brainstorm "kitchen table" style, in which you sit around casually with friends and say, "Hey, let's tell stories about times when we . . ." It starts off slowly and eventually explodes as memory triggers memory and one theme leads to another. It is helpful to take some time at the end of the session to write down a word or two (like those on the brainstorm list) to describe each memory that surfaced for you during this session.

Once you have the brainstorm list you can refer to it to develop memories into more complete stories for your own learning, and or for telling to others. The process of developing a memory into a story is a wonderful creative process that often proves to be not just fun but very therapeutic.

When it seems appropriate, you may wish to retell the story of the week as if it had happened to you.

Trying on the Ideas in the Story. In this section I offer creative suggestions for trying out the ways of seeing, thinking, and being that are reflected in the stories. These can be practiced throughout your week. These ideas are responses to my personal interpretations; I hope you will experiment with the ones that feel right to you or create your own. I realize that in our busy lives it is hard to follow through on many things as much as we would like, but the planting of seeds does bear fruit. Apply your creativity here; make use of the metaphors, let this be a form of play.

Sharing the Story with Others. I encourage you to share the stories with others. This may well be the most rewarding aspect of using this book. You may photocopy (one copy only please) a story a week and put it on your refrigerator or desk, or office bulletin board. Starting a lunch chat group or an Internet chat group using the stories may interest you.

Stories are meant to be shared. If the story moves you at all, tell it to someone else. Try telling it in your own words. Parables and folktales are meant to be told. Folktales have always been just that: wisdom passed from folk to folk, changing to suit the time and place and needs of the listener and the teller. When we let go of the written text and tell a story in our own words, we bring forth what is powerful in it for us.

It is important that you do not try to memorize a story word for word. Memorizing can create anxiety, making the words more powerful than the ideas and images they carry. All you need to learn by heart is the basic sequence of events. When this is familiar to you, the story will flow in your own words and images. I have intentionally included very short stories here to enable easy learning and sharing.

My students and I use these four steps in learning a story:

1. Write a simple outline of the main events of the story in order, committing only the order to memory. For example: (a) Little Red Riding Hood sets off for Granny's house with goodies. (b) She

meets a wolf in the woods. (c) The wolf takes a shortcut. (d) The wolf eats Granny, puts on her clothes, and gets into bed. (e) Etc.

2. Tell the basic story to someone without attempts at dramatization, and without looking at your outline or text to see if you remember the main sequence of events. How you tell it—the things you remember and what you forget—helps you see what is important to you about the story.

3. Close your eyes and walk through the story, using all of your senses to ground it in a place and time, and to bring it to life using your own imagery. A good time to do this is at night when you first get into bed, if you are not too tired, or any time when you can close your eyes and focus quietly.

4. Practice retelling the story by yourself or with a partner, adding imagery, movement, voice, and characters which feel appropriate and comfortable. There is no right way to tell a story. Everyone has their own style based on their individual strengths and skills and interests. Remember, if a story is told well, it is the story that stands out rather than the storyteller.

You will find that some of these suggestions work well for you and others do not. Find what is good for you. Above all, take the time to contemplate: How is this my story?

Creating a Personal Vision to Guide Your Journey

As I worked on this book, reading and rereading each story and contemplating them in the ways that I have suggested, it became clear to me that I needed to have a stronger vision of my spiritual goals. Without this vision I was in danger of trying on one idea after another in a willy-nilly fashion without a sense of wholeness or clear purpose. There are so many people offering so many great ideas about what we need to do in order to awaken to enlightenment. If we do not have a vision of what we desire or imagine, we will constantly be pulled this way and that, not necessarily finding what is right for us.

Therefore, before you read any of the stories, I encourage you to take the time to describe your image of your ideal self, your highest aspiration. You may not know how to get where you are going, but you do know where you would like to end up and can work backwards from there. You might start by writing a description of why you are here on this planet, what you hope to learn, and how you would be if you lived most closely to those goals. This is a vision of how you will be in the world, more than what you will do. This vision can take a number of forms:

1. A spiritual eulogy that you would like to have read at your funeral.
2. A letter written from your most evolved self to you, describing who you really are at core, and what your healing path will be.
3. A description of yourself at some point, say two, five, or ten years in the future.
4. You may wish to express this through some form other than writing, such as a dance or a painting or telling it as a story, so that you step into the vision as much as possible.

Your vision may include the work that you would like to do, as long as you can see how your spiritual development will enhance it. Be specific. The more clearly you can see, hear, touch, taste, smell, and feel yourself living and being in this expanded state, the more you will be reminded to step into it daily.

Share your vision with someone you trust. You will be pleased to discover that you are a lot closer in many aspects to this ideal image than you give yourself credit for. Sharing it with others also helps you to commit to it.

Once you have written down this self-image, put it somewhere safe and refer to it often.

STORY WATER

A
story is like water
that you heat for your bath.

It takes messages between the fire
and your skin. It lets them meet,
and it cleans you!

Very few can sit down
in the middle of the fire itself
like a salamander or Abraham.
We need intermediaries.

A feeling of fullness comes,
but usually it takes some bread
to bring it.

Beauty surrounds us,
but usually we need to be walking
in a garden to know it.

The body itself is a screen
to shield and partially reveal
the light that's blazing
inside your presence.

Water, stories, the body,
all things we do, are mediums
that hide and show what's hidden.

Study them,
and enjoy this being washed
with a secret we sometimes know,
and then not.

—*Jelaluddin Rumi*

THE MONK AND THE SCORPION

B u d d h i s t

Once a monk sat on the banks of the Ganges River with one of his students. As they watched the water flow by, a large scorpion making its way along the steep banks fell into the water and began to struggle and drown. Without hesitation, the monk reached in and pulled the scorpion from the water. As he placed it on the bank it stung his hand.

Several minutes later this same scorpion fell again into the river and commenced to drown. Again the monk reached in and again was stung as he set the scorpion on the bank.

A third time the scorpion fell and a third time it was retrieved by the monk with the same results.

The student could no longer restrain himself. "Master," he asked, "why is it that you keep saving that beastly scorpion from drowning? Can't you see that it is just going to sting you?"

"Yes, I know it is going to sting me," laughed the monk. "It is the dharma of a scorpion to sting. But it is my dharma to save."

YOUR STORY
Explore the story through meditation, visualization, writing, and/or an expressive art form.

MAKING A PERSONAL CONNECTION WITH THE STORY
The monk in this story said "It is my dharma to save," and he applied that knowledge to the everyday aspects of his life despite the pain he knew he might feel. What is your dharma or your highest vision for

yourself as a positive force in the world? What goals or dreams do you have for yourself that you hope to do, "when you grow up"? Tell yourself these stories in rich detail, perhaps as a visualization with eyes closed as a waking dream.

What are the scorpions that threaten to sting you? How can you gather the courage to be who you want to be, and do what you long to do, in spite of the sting or the fear of the sting? Add this element to your story.

Brainstorm a list of times in which you acted out of your highest desire, or dharma. Then develop one or several of these stories, exploring how you felt. Telling these stories to yourself reminds you of your own courage and passion, and inspires you for future action.

Brainstorm a list of times when you did not act out of your desire or dharma. Then develop one or several of these stories. Explore how you felt and what the scorpions were that held you back.

If you have not already done so, you might like to write out your vision of yourself living your dharma.

TRYING ON THE IDEAS IN THE STORY

As you go about your week, notice the impulses that you have to help, or to interact, or to speak your mind, or to create, and notice what inhibits you from doing so.

SHARING THE STORY WITH OTHERS

Share this story with others. Then share personal stories, in "kitchen-table" style, of following and not following your dharma. Oh, those scorpions!

THE GOOD SAMARITAN

Christian

In the parable of the good Samaritan, a lawyer asks Jesus what he must do to attain eternal life. Jesus reminds him of the commandment as it is written, that the lawyer must love not only God but also "your neighbor as yourself." The lawyer, seeking to justify his actions, asks for clarification of exactly who constitutes a neighbor that he must treat lovingly.

Jesus replied, "A Jewish man was going down from Jerusalem to Jericho, and fell into the hands of robbers, who stripped him, and beat him, and went away, leaving him half dead. Now by chance a Jewish priest was going down that road; and when he saw him, he passed by on the other side. So likewise a Levite, when he came to the place and saw him, passed by on the other side.

"But a Samaritan (a mixed blood race despised by the Jews), while traveling came near him; and when he saw him, he was moved with pity. He went to him and bandaged up his wounds, pouring oil and wine on them. Then he put him on his own animal, brought him to an inn, and took care of him. The next day he took out two denarii, gave them to the innkeeper, and said, 'Take care of him; and when I come back, I will repay you whatever more you spend.'

"Which of these three, do you think, was a neighbor to the man who fell into the hands of robbers?" asked Jesus.

The lawyer replied, "The one who showed him mercy." Jesus said to him, "Go and do likewise."

YOUR STORY

Explore the story through meditation, visualization, writing, and/or an expressive art form.

MAKING A PERSONAL CONNECTION WITH THE STORY

It is surprising what a sense of joy can come from helping someone, whether a stranger or a loved one. Write about or share a time when you helped a stranger. Can you think of a time when you "passed by on the other side"? Write about or share a time when a stranger or acquaintance helped you.

Some questions to ask yourself: What is it like to love and help strangers? Who are your neighbors and who are not? Jesus said to love your neighbor as yourself. How much do you love yourself? Loving and accepting ourselves as we are is the first step toward being able to see all others with true compassion.

TRYING ON THE IDEAS IN THE STORY

This week, try behaving toward everyone you meet as the Samaritan treated the man on the road. See if you can act on your impulses to extend a hand more often.

Try treating yourself the way you believe a loving being like Jesus or Buddha, Mohammed, Mother Teresa, or the Bal Shem Tov (or your personal favorite) would treat you.

SHARING THE STORIES WITH OTHERS

This is a rich story for sharing "helping and not-helping" experiences with others.

three

"THAT IS GOOD"

India

L ong ago in India a king ruled the land. Always by his side was his minister, who was known for his wisdom, but also for a strange habit that often annoyed the king. For no matter what happened, he always responded by saying, "That is good, that is good."

One day the king was out hunting when his horse was startled by a large snake. The king was thrown from the horse and dragged some distance, in the process deeply cutting his foot and losing a toe. As his minister knelt beside him to inspect the damage he said, "That is good, that is good."

"How can you say that is good?" the king screamed in outrage. "What kind of minister are you? You are dismissed from your post immediately."

"That is good," said the minister, "that is good," and off he went to the palace to pack his bags.

The king returned home and his foot eventually healed, minus the toe. Again one day he decided to go hunting. This time he became separated from his hunting party. Suddenly he was ambushed by the tribal people who lived near those woods. He was tied up and taken back to their village.

Now these tribal people had a custom of sacrificing their prisoners (the king in this case) to their god. They prepared him for the sacrificial celebration, washing and decorating him. The celebration began with music and dancing as he was led to the slaughtering place like a goat. The king shook with terror from head to foot. He nearly fainted when the priest came forward waving a long knife. The priest danced around him, inspecting him from every angle. Suddenly he motioned for the music and dancing to stop. "This one is no good," he said. "He has been cut." He pointed to the missing toe. "We cannot sacrifice to God something that has already been cut." The priest slashed at the vines that bound the king's hands and legs, and set him free. The king limped back to the palace as quickly as he could.

Once back in the safety of his palace, the king remembered his minister and called for him. He told him the story and said, "You were right. It was good that my toe was lost. Because of it, I was not sacrificed by the tribal people. But why did you say 'This is good' when I fired you from your post?"

"There is always some good to come out of things, your highness," replied the minister. "If I had not been fired, I would have been with you that day when you were captured by the tribal people. Because I have all of my toes, I would have been next in line for the sacrifice."

"You are truly right, my friend," said the king. "That was good, that was good indeed, and so is your wisdom. You shall advise me always." And he did. And it was good.

~ ~ ~

Your Story

Explore the story through meditation, visualization, writing, and/or an expressive art form.

Making a Personal Connection with the Story

What meaning does this story have for you? Brainstorm a list of experiences which seemed at first to be bad luck, then later proved to be fortunate or at least good learning experiences. Develop one or several of these into a story that can be shared with others and can be a good reminder to yourself.

Trying on the Ideas in the Story

Let the king's minister be your guide this week. Carry him on your shoulder. Give him a voice. When the urge to judge events comes up, say: "There must be some higher good that I cannot foresee." Or ask, "What can I learn from this?" Or simply say, "That is good!" Notice how this changes the way that you experience your day-to-day world.

You can also discover the good in events by taking the time to write the day's happenings in a journal, and reflecting on them at the end of the week.

Sharing the Story with Others

Take a risk, give the minister a fun voice and character.

Make up your own modern-day version of the story.

four

ABOU BEN ADHEM

Leigh Hunt

Abou Ben Adhem (may his tribe increase!)
Awoke one night from a deep dream of peace,
and saw within the moonlight in his room,
making it rich, and like a lily in bloom,
an angel writing in a book of gold:
exceeding peace had made Ben Adhem bold,
and to the presence in the room he said,
"What writest thou?"—The vision raised its head,
and with a look made of all sweet accord,
answered, "The names of those who love the lord."
"And is mine one?" said Abou. "Nay, not so,"
replied the angel. Abou spoke more low,
but cheerily still; and said, "I pray thee, then,
write me as one that loves his fellow-men."
The angel wrote, and vanished. The next night
it came again with a great awakening light,
and showed the names whom love of God had blessed,
and lo! Ben Adhem's name led all the rest!

YOUR STORY
Explore the story through meditation, visualization, writing, and/or an expressive art form.

MAKING A PERSONAL CONNECTION WITH THE STORY
What meaning does this story poem have for you? Would your name be written in the book of those who loved their fellow human beings?

Tell your own stories about experiences in which you have felt great love for your fellow humans.

The experience of loving others is perhaps the most profound experience of our lives. Remember times of great love and try to regenerate those feelings in your heart.

TRYING ON THE IDEAS IN THE STORY

Mother Teresa suggested that we love each human being we encounter as if they were God, Jesus, Allah, or whoever we worship. What would it take for you to see God in each person you meet? Try this for one week. The Buddhist salutation *namaste* means, roughly, "I honor that which is God-like in you, or that place where you and I are one." Try saying that to yourself as you greet or see people. Remember the strong feelings of love you feel or have felt and share them with others.

SHARING THE STORY WITH OTHERS

Poems do require memorization if they are to be shared without reading. This can be well worth the effort because once learned, they are not easily forgotten. If you are going to read them aloud, read over them a few times first for proper expression.

Write your own narrative poem about your love for your fellow human beings.

f i v e

LEAVE YOUR NAME ON THE DOOR

M i d d l e   E a s t

A philosopher, having made an appointment to dispute with Nasrudin, called at the appointed hour and found him away from home. Nasrudin had forgotten their plan and was in the teahouse playing table games and telling stories with his friends.

After waiting for some time the philosopher grew angry. Picking up a piece of chalk, he wrote "Stupid Oaf" on Nasrudin's door and left in a huff.

As soon as he got home and saw this, Nasrudin rushed to the philosopher's house.

"I had completely forgotten our appointment," he said, "I apologize for not having been home. Of course, I remembered the appointment as soon as I saw that you had left your name on my door."

Nasrudin the Hodja is said to have been a real person born in Turkey in the year 1208. Hodja means teacher, and Nasrudin was a teacher/wise man and sometimes a judge. He was also all too human, and it is his humanness that inspires much of the humor in his stories. He lived at the time of the powerful conqueror Tamerlane and is said to have won him over through cleverness and humor.

He is said to have died around 1284. Even in death he makes one laugh and pause to wonder. His grave is marked by a single iron gate. The gate is locked—but there are no walls on either side.

Since his death the people of Turkey and many other countries in the Middle East have been telling stories about him. Some may be true; others surely are made up, inspired by his character. Stories are still being made in his name today. Custom has it that when you tell one tale about Nasrudin you must tell another: More to the point, one cannot help but tell another.

YOUR STORY
Explore the story through meditation, visualization, writing, and/or an expressive art form.

MAKING A PERSONAL CONNECTION WITH THE STORY
The way we treat others will ultimately tell about who we are. What names do you leave on doors? In this story a person's wounded ego caused him to behave in a mean way. Can you describe situations in which you have acted like the angry philosopher? Describe situations in which others have treated you this way. How did they make you feel?

TRYING ON THE STORY IDEAS
As you go about your week, notice how you describe yourself in the way that you treat others. Make an effort to leave your highest, most sacred name on all the doors you pass through.

Just for fun you might pick that sacred name for yourself and write it on your own door just to see how people react to you.

SHARING THE STORY WITH OTHERS
This story always gets a quick, hearty laugh as listeners recognize the wisdom in it. Sometimes very short stories feel awkward because they end so abruptly with a punch line. As with telling a joke, it is helpful to memorize the last line so that you feel comfortable enough to deliver it smoothly.

six

SPEAK ONLY PRAISE

Hasidic

The Chafetz Chaim (Rabbi Israel Meir HaCohen) dedicated his life to teaching, preaching, and writing about the gravity of gossip, slander and evil talk.

Once, on a train returning from a trip, he met another traveler. "Where are you heading?" asked the Chafetz Chaim.

"I am on my way to Radin to see the great tzaddik, the Chafetz Chaim," the man said.

The Chafetz Chaim, who was a paragon of humility, asked, "Why do you call him a great tzaddik? What is so special about him? He is a person like any other."

"How dare you speak with such insolence about the great tzaddik!" the man said, accompanying his rebuke with a sound slap to the sage's face.

Upon being introduced to the Chafetz Chaim in Radin, the embarrassed man asked forgiveness for his rudeness.

"There is no need to apologize," said the Chafetz Chaim. "After all, it was my honor you were defending. But this incident taught me something valuable. You must not speak badly of any person, even of yourself."

~ ~ ~

YOUR STORY
Explore the story through meditation, visualization, writing, and/or an expressive art form.

MAKING A PERSONAL CONNECTION WITH THE STORY
Our words have power—they can create or they can be damaging. If we follow the Buddhist admonition to do no harm, we must apply this to ourselves as well. Retell the story with yourself as the main charac-

ter and someone who respects you as the other character. How else could you have responded to the praise in your name? Women especially have been socialized to view their talents and abilities as insignificant. Imagine what it feels like to honor yourself fully in another's presence in a way that feels good to you.

TRYING ON THE IDEAS IN THE STORY

As you go about your week, listen to how you speak of yourself to others, and to yourself. If you hear yourself putting yourself down, however subtly or humorously, reframe your statement to be a positive, compassionate one. Practice saying "Thank you" without qualification when you are given a compliment of any sort.

A worthwhile exercise to try each morning is to acknowledge, either in writing or prayer, three things that you like about yourself.

SHARING THE STORY WITH OTHERS

Share personal versions of this story as well as the original one.

seven

THE CRICKET STORY

Contemporary North American

Once two friends were walking down the sidewalk of a busy city street during rush hour. There was all sorts of noise in the city; car horns honking, feet shuffling, people talking! And amid all this noise, one of the friends turned to the other and said, "I hear a cricket."

"No way," her friend responded. "How could you possibly hear a cricket with all of this noise? You must be imagining it. Besides, I've never seen a cricket in the city."

"No, really, I do hear a cricket. I'll show you." She stopped for a moment, then led her friend across the street to a big cement planter with a tree in it. Pushing back some leaves she found a little brown cricket.

"That's amazing!" said her friend. "You must have super-human hearing. What's your secret?"

"No, my hearing is just the same as yours. There's no secret," the first woman replied. "Watch, I'll show you." She reached into her pocket, pulled out some loose change, and threw it on the sidewalk. Amid all the noise of the city, everyone within thirty feet turned their head to see where the sound of the money was coming from.

"See," she said. "It's all a matter of what you are listening for."

~ ~ ~

YOUR STORY

Explore the story through meditation, visualization, writing, and/or an expressive art form.

Making a Personal Connection with the Story

The character in the story listened for the sounds of nature even on a busy city street, and she found them. What things are you aware of? What are you looking for? Can you describe experiences in which you noticed things amid the hubbub of life? What things have you missed?

Trying on the Ideas in the Story

Think about something you did during your day that did not require all of your concentration, such as walking down a street, driving, or eating. Close your eyes and try to remember what you focused on and noticed, and what you tuned out.

As you go about your week, notice what you focus on and what you filter out. Try shifting your focus to things that nurture, such as natural surroundings or the God-likeness in the eyes, voice, and kindness of others. Look for beauty. Surround yourself with the beauty that is there.

Sharing the Story with Others

Share this with a group and go on a treasure hunt for beautiful things.

e i g h t

THE DERVISH IN THE DITCH

S u f i

O nce a Dervish holy man and his student were walking down a long, quiet road. Suddenly they saw dust rising in the distance. A fine carriage pulled by six horses approached at full gallop. The men soon realized that this carriage was not going to slow down or veer to avoid them. In fact it was coming upon them at such speed that they had to throw themselves from the road, landing quite unceremoniously in a ditch. The two men got up as quickly as they could and looked back at the carriage as it sped by.

The student thought to curse, but not before the teacher ran after them calling: "May all of your deepest desires be satisfied!"

"Why would you wish something so good for those men?" the student asked. "They just forced us into the ditch, we could have been hurt."

"Do you really think," replied the teacher, "that if their deepest desires were satisfied, they would go around treating others as they treated us?"

JESUS' PURSE

s u f i

A Sufi writer once said of Jesus that sometimes people would make fun of him or curse him aloud, but that he would always answer back with prayers in their names. On one such occasion his disciples asked him how he could not be angry and want to curse those people.

They asked him how he could pray for those who had harmed him.

Jesus answered them by saying that he "could only spend of what he had in his purse."

Your Story

Explore the stories through meditation, visualization, writing, and/or an expressive art form.

Making a Personal Connection with the Story

In the first story the Dervish responds to the action of the protagonists with vision and compassion. His student's response is ruled by his ego. Tell the story of a situation in which your ego ruled your response. Tell the story of a time when your response was ruled by vision and compassion.

According to this Sufi writer, Jesus had nothing but love inside, and so that was all he could give to others. What is in your purse? What would it take to have nothing but love inside?

Trying on the Ideas in the Story

Notice what is in your purse as you go about your week. Try carrying only love and see how that affects what you give to others. When things happen to annoy or upset you, try answering the way these two teachers would.

Sharing the Story with Others

These stories are small enough to fit even into the smallest wallet. Sometimes a really short story with a punch line can end almost too quickly. Try to read your listeners' faces after telling them these stories. I find it helps some listeners if you repeat the final line of the story, using different words. In "Jesus' Purse," try ending with something like "he had only love in his purse so that was all he could give to those who assaulted him."

nine

HOW THE SPIDER SYMBOL CAME
TO THE PEOPLE

Osage Plains Indians

One day the chief of the Isolated Earth People was hunting in the forest. He was hunting for a symbol to give life to his people, some great and powerful animal that would show itself to him and teach him an important lesson. As he hunted he spied the tracks of a huge deer. The chief became very excited.

"Grandfather deer," he said, "surely you are going to show yourself to me. You are going to teach me a lesson and become one of the symbols of my people."

The chief began following the deer's tracks. His eyes were on nothing else, and he went faster and faster through the forest. Suddenly the chief ran right into a huge spider's web that had been strung across between the trees. It made him stumble. When he got to his feet he was angry. He struck at the spider, but the spider dodged aside and climbed out of reach.

"Grandson," the spider said, "why do you run through the woods looking at nothing but the ground? Why do you act as if you were blind?"

The chief answered, "I was following the tracks of a great deer. I am seeking a symbol to give life and strength to my people."

"I can be such a symbol," said the spider.

"How could you give strength to my people?" the chief asked. "You are small and weak and I didn't even see you."

"Grandson," said the spider, "look upon me. I am patient. I watch and I wait. Then all things come to me. If your people learn this, they will be strong indeed."

The chief saw that it was so, and the spider became one of the symbols of the Osage people.

~~~   ~~~   ~~~

Your Story

Explore the story through meditation, visualization, writing, and/or an expressive art form.

Making a Personal Connection with the Story

What meaning does this story have for you? Retell the story with yourself as the main character. What symbol would you be looking for? How would cultivating the qualities of the spider change your life and spiritual quest? What totem animal would you like to find? How would cultivating the qualities of the animal of your choice affect your life?

Trying on the Ideas in the Story

Make a list of the qualities of a spider. As you go through your week, notice opportunities for cultivating patience and watchfulness and any other qualities you have on your list. Take some time to emulate the spider, at work, at home, out in nature, or at the mall.

Sharing the Story with Others

Help people to create stories in which their own totem animal offers specific qualities and insights that they can learn from. Kids love this exercise.

t e n

"THIS, TOO, SHALL PASS"

The Talmud

King Solomon was wise and powerful with riches beyond compare, and yet he was not content. "I am too often depressed by life," he told his wise men. "If things go my way, I do not trust that it will last. If they do not, I fear my woes will never end. I have dreamt that there is a ring that contains the knowledge that will bring me peace of mind. Please go and find me this ring. I wish to have it by Succoth, six months from now."

The king's advisers each went their own way, asking in each place for this marvelous, powerful ring that would bring their king peace of mind. They went to the finest jewelers and goldsmiths in Jerusalem and described the magic qualities of the ring, but no one had heard of it. They traveled to Damascus, Babylon, and Tyre and spoke to traders and merchants who had traveled the seas, but no one had heard of such a ring. They traveled to Egypt and many other places, but met with no success.

Many times the king asked them if they had found the ring, and they had to reply, "Not yet, your highness." Solomon's hope was fading.

Six months passed. On the last night before Succoth eve the advisers still had not found the ring. They had given up, all save one, the youngest. Unable to sleep, he walked through the city streets all night. In the morning he found himself on a street with the very poorest houses. He saw an old man setting out his simple jewelry and trinkets for sale. In one last attempt he described the ring to this man.

The old man was quiet for a while, and then he smiled. He went inside his simple dwelling and returned with a plain gold ring. With a sharp tool he engraved something on it and laid it in the adviser's hand. As the wise man read what was written on the ring his heart filled with joy. "This is the ring!" he exclaimed. He gave the old man all the money he had and hurried back to the palace. That evening at the Succoth feast King Solomon silenced the crowd. "Advisers, have you found me the ring of my dream?" he asked. "We have, your highness," spoke the youngest. He came forward and placed the ring on King Solomon's hand. The king looked at the ring and read the Hebrew words engraved there: Gam Zeh Ya'avor—"This, too, shall pass." As he read, the king's sorrows turned to joy, and his joys to sorrow, and then both gave way to peace. The king was reminded in that moment that all his riches and glory were impermanent, and all his sorrows would pass away as the seasons and the years.

From that time on, King Solomon wore the ring and was reminded, in good times and bad, that "This, too, shall pass."

YOUR STORY
Explore the story through meditation, visualization, writing, and/or an expressive art form.

MAKING A PERSONAL CONNECTION WITH THE STORY
What meaning does this story have for you?

As King Solomon put on the ring he realized that his power and his pain were impermanent. So too all of our problems and our triumphs are impermanent. Can you tell stories of times in your life when this wisdom could have lessened your unhappiness?

TRYING ON THE IDEAS IN THE STORY
Make yourself a ring out of masking tape or something that you can write on and inscribe it with the words "This, too, shall pass" or the initials "TTSP" or the Yiddish acronym "GZY." Wear your homemade ring this week and see if your reactions to the experiences of your life are affected.

SHARING THE STORY WITH OTHERS

Help others to make rings. At the end of the week share your ring stories. To all who ask about the ring, you can tell the story.

eleven

THE BUNDLE OF STICKS

Aesop

An aging farmer lay on his deathbed thinking about the welfare of his family. His three sons could not see eye to eye, they quarreled day and night. What, he worried, would become of his family? He had tried speaking with them about the importance of forgiving and forgetting and living in peace, but they ignored his words and grew more bitter by the day.

Finally, as his strength waned, the old man had an idea. He called his sons to his bedside, asking the eldest to bring a bundle of sticks.

"Now, my sons," he said, "I want you to break this bundle in two."

The first son tried, and then the second, and finally the third. But no matter how hard they tried, they could not break the bundle of sticks.

"Now untie it," said the farmer. "Each of you take one and try to break it."

The sticks broke easily in the hands of each of the three sons.

"You are like these sticks, my sons," said the father. "If you stick together, no one and no thing will be able to harm you, but if you quarrel and divide yourselves, your enemies will destroy you."

YOUR STORY
Explore the story through meditation, visualization, writing, and/or an expressive art form.

Making a Personal Connection with the Story

Brainstorm a list of experiences in which you stuck together with others: family, friends, co-workers, community members, or like-minded people united for a common gain. Brainstorm a list of times in which you were disconnected from family, friends, community members, or co-workers. How did you feel? Imagine a scenario in which you mend past differences and work together with others.

Are there people in your life against whom you hold grudges or anger or hatred? Forgiving others does not mean forgetting what hurt us. It means acknowledging the circumstances that led others to behave badly. Forgiveness also means letting go of the anger we may hold against ourselves for having been vulnerable enough to be victim to another's rage, selfishness, or fear. Forgiveness allows us to have a deeper relationship with ourselves and with others.

This theme can also be applied on a cultural and political level. Are there people in your cultural or religious or ethnic group with whom you battle? What can you do together that you cannot do divided? Do you keep a distance from those who hold different political or religious views? Can you see how this widens the gap?

Make a list of the people from whom you are divided or against whom you hold a grudge or feel anger. Look at your anger in this new light. Can you forgive yourself? Can you forgive them? How does it feel?

Trying on the Ideas in the Story

Go gather some sticks and try this for yourself. As you go about your week, look for situations in which the story could serve you as suggested below.

Sharing the Stories with Others

This story offers a clear metaphor. Is there someone with whom you could share the story and perhaps a stick (a.k.a. olive branch)? Give the story out as a present or holiday card. If you are working on a particular cause and you have differences with others, try to decide whether your differences are really greater than your shared vision. Tell the story at a work meeting or family gathering and pass out sticks to each person. Have fun with a difficult subject in this way!

t w e l v e

CATCH THE WIND

Desert   Fathers

A brother came to abbot pastor and said, "Many distracting thoughts come into my mind, and I am in danger because of them." Then the elder thrust him out into the open air and said, "Open up the garments about your chest and catch the wind in them." But he replied, "This I cannot do." So the elder said to him, "If you cannot catch the wind, neither can you prevent distracting thoughts from coming into your head. Your job is to say 'No' to them."

DO NOT OPEN THE DOOR

Hasidic

A student once asked his rabbi for help. "I try to study and pray," he said, "but distracting, troubling thoughts are always coming into my head and I cannot control them."

"What would you do," asked the rabbi, "if you saw from your window that a person was coming to your home whom you did not wish to talk with? Would you let him in?"

"I would not open the door. I would tell them to go away," the student replied.

"Exactly," said the rabbi. "You must be aware of thoughts when they are at your mind's door and simply turn them away."

YOUR STORY

Explore the stories through visualization, writing, and/or an expressive art form.

MAKING A PERSONAL CONNECTION WITH THE STORIES

In both of these stories the teacher helps the student understand that the mind has "distracting" thoughts. The student is not to blame for them, but can stop them from dominating his or her mind. Being aware of the thoughts that come into our minds and determining whether or not we want these thoughts to remain is called mindfulness, or attentiveness. There are many techniques for practicing such attentiveness and ultimately cultivating a quiet mind. See the suggestions in the bibliography for books on starting or enhancing a meditation practice.

TRYING ON THE IDEAS IN THE STORY

This week be aware, whether in meditation or not, of what is going through your mind. Even if you cannot quiet your mind, you can shorten the length of time you spend caught in a fantasy involving something in the past or future. These fantasies are stories. Learn about yourself by observing the kind of memories, thoughts, and fantasies that preoccupy you. You can choose to say no to these dramas that are shaping your reality. Just as you would change the TV channel, you can consciously turn to a different thought.

Throughout your week, pick "anchor points" that will remind you to return to the present moment and to a quiet mind, times such as having a cup of tea, going to the bathroom, walking outside, eating dinner, hanging up the phone.

An example of one such exercise, taken from Lawrence LeShan's *How to Meditate,* is to imagine yourself sitting at the bottom of a river. As thoughts come, look at them or ignore them, and then let them go up and away in a bubble. Then return to quiet peacefulness.

SHARING THE STORIES WITH OTHERS

These anecdotes can serve as helpful guides for a meditation group or before silent prayer in a place of worship.

t h i r t e e n

WHAT IS HEAVEN, WHAT IS HELL

Z e n

Once a samurai came to the master Hakuin and asked, "Master, tell me, is there really such a thing as heaven and hell?"

The master was quiet for quite some time while gazing at the man. "Who are you?" he asked at last.

"I am a samurai swordsman, and a member of the emperor's personal guard."

"You a samurai!" said Hakuin doubtfully. "What kind of emperor would have you for a guard? You look more like a beggar!"

"What?" the samurai stammered, growing red in the face and reaching for his sword.

"Oho!" said Hakuin. "So you have a sword, do you! I'll bet it's much too dull to cut off my head!"

The samurai could no longer contain himself. He drew his sword and readied to strike the master.

Hakuin responded quickly, "That is hell!"

The samurai, understanding the truth in the master's words and the risk he had taken, sheathed his sword and bowed. "Now," said the master, "That is heaven."

YOUR STORY

Explore the story through meditation, visualization, writing, and/or an expressive art form.

MAKING A PERSONAL CONNECTION WITH THE STORY

Why did the samurai raise his sword against the master? Why did he bow? One interpretation of the samurai's response is that he was let-

ting his ego rule him. Brainstorm a list of times when you have responded
to a situation with your ego. Brainstorm a list of times in which you put
your ego aside and responded with your heart. How did these feel different? How were the outcomes different?

TRYING ON THE IDEAS IN THE STORY

As you go about your week, be aware of when your ego rules versus when
your heart rules. See how often you can invoke heaven and avoid hell by
actually bowing to the stresses and problems that trouble your mind, releas-
ing ego and opening the way for heart. Bowing physically or in your imagination will solidify the image for you.

SHARING THE STORY WITH OTHERS

Create your own modern version of this story, or tell a brief personal version as an addendum to the traditional tale.

f o u r t e e n

THE BURIED TREASURE

S u f i

Once a farmer lay on his deathbed despairing of the fate of his lazy sons. Near his final hour, an inspiration came to him. He called his sons around his bedside and bade them draw in close. "I am soon to leave this world, my sons," he whispered. "I want you to know that I have left a treasure of gold for you. I have hidden it in my field. Dig carefully and well and you shall find it. I ask only that you share it amongst yourselves evenly."

The sons begged him to tell them *exactly* where he had buried it, but the father breathed his last breath and spoke no more.

As soon as their father was buried, the sons took up their pitchforks and shovels and began to turn over the soil in their father's field. They dug and dug until they had turned over the whole field twice. They found no treasure. But they decided that since the field was so well dug up they might as well plant some grain as their father had done. The crop grew well for them. After the harvest they decided to dig again in hopes of finding the buried treasure. Again they found not a treasure, but a field prepared for sowing. This year's crop was better than the one before.

This went on for a number of years until the sons had grown accustomed to the cycles of the seasons and the rewards of daily labor. By that time their farming earned them each enough money to live a happy life. It was then that they realized the treasure their father had left for them.

Your Story

Explore the story through meditation, visualization, writing, and/or an expressive art form.

Making a Personal Connection with the Story

Who among us has not wished for buried treasure to make our lives easier? Miracles do happen. But often we wish for a miracle because we can't see any other way to get what we think we need. How many of us, if we knew with certainty that we could have what we desired, would not work for it step by step, one day at a time?

It can seem so overwhelming to imagine the changes that many of us wish to make in our lives, whether a change in our physical being or a change in our relational lives, our material lives or our spiritual lives. Yet the way most of us actually do get to where we want to be is one step at a time. These men had the vision of gold to keep them digging. If they had just gotten the money to begin with, they never would have discovered the beauty of the seasons and the satisfaction of creativity, or the skills necessary to bring about a steady income.

Taking small daily steps toward our desired way of being is the best way to achieve success. Tell stories of the ways that you have grown as a human being through daily study and toil.

Trying on the Ideas in the Story

Dr. Andrew Weil's book *Eight Weeks to Optimum Health* has been enormously popular because it teaches people how to improve their health gradually in small, manageable ways, like adding a ten-minute walk a day or an extra helping of broccoli each week, rather than sweeping changes which are too disruptive to our lifestyles to maintain. What would your spiritual equivalents of small steps to growth be? Could it include things like a walk in a quiet, natural place, even if only for ten minutes a day? A moment of quiet before dinner? Writing a two-line poem before bed? Calling someone you love once a week and telling them so? Sending five dollars to a cause you believe in but hadn't supported? Make your own list and try out one or two things at a time.

Visualize the changes you are hoping for as having happened in your life. Rewind the visualization slowly, seeing the steps that it would take to get you to the end point.

Acknowledge in writing all of the unexpected "miracles" that have happened when things didn't go the way you thought they should. Write also about the things you have learned through work and study.

SHARING THE STORY WITH OTHERS

These stories can inspire treasure hunts that families or co-workers could work on together.

f i f t e e n

THE PEDDLER OF SWAFFHAM

E n g l a n d

Once in Swaffham in Norfolk, a peddler named Chapman lived in a small house beside a towering oak tree. One night the peddler dreamed that there came a knock on his door. When he opened it there stood a saintly messenger. The messenger told him that if he went to London Bridge he would find a treasure. He didn't go right away, but after the dream had visited him several nights, he packed his things and walked all the way to London Bridge. There he stood upon the bridge for three days looking about and listening for some news of his treasure.

At last a shopkeeper who had been watching the peddler came out to him. "I've been watching you for three days, standing here on the bridge neither selling wares nor seeking alms," said the shopkeeper. "I beg you tell me what is your business."

The peddler told the shopkeeper about his dream.

The shopkeeper laughed. "What a fool you are, taking such a long journey for the sake of a dream! Peddler, last night I had a dream that I was supposed to go to Swaffham in Norfolk, a place completely foreign to me. I dreamed that I was to go behind a small house owned by a fellow named Chapman. Next to the house was a towering oak tree. I dreamed that if I dug under that tree I would find a vast treasure. Now, you don't see me running off to Swaffham just because of some foolish dream, do you? Were I you, I'd get myself home again."

Chapman thanked the man for his wise advice and set off immediately for home. There he dug under the great oak and found a large box, filled with a vast treasure indeed.

~~~   ~~~   ~~~

YOUR STORY

Explore the story through meditation, visualization, writing, and/or an expressive art form.

MAKING A PERSONAL CONNECTION WITH THE STORY

The peddler eventually trusts his dreams and is guided home to the treasure in his own backyard. Changing the symbolism to suit your life, retell this story as if you were the main character. What are your deepest dreams or desires? Think for a minute as if your dreams or aspirations were your greatest treasure. What would you do right now if you could do anything in the world? What treasures would this lead you to?

What does it mean to you to follow your dreams? How well do you listen to your intuition or inner voice?

TRYING ON THE IDEAS IN THE STORY

As you go through your week, consult your inner wisdom before you act. Notice when you are seeking treasures that others have told you are valuable and when you are valuing the treasures that live in you.

Sometimes we take the treasures in our lives for granted, focusing instead on what we lack. William Blake said, "Gratitude is heaven itself." Take time this week to make a list each night of all the things and experiences that you have to be thankful for. Include a list of your personal qualities that are treasures, and take the time to celebrate them.

SHARING THE STORY WITH OTHERS

Share this story, as well as your own stories of grace, with others.

sixteen

GOD SENDS A LIFEBOAT

Contemporary   North   American

Once upon a time, not too long ago and not so far away, there lived a very devout man of the cloth. Now one year in his area there were tremendous rains that turned into a flood. A dam burst in a nearby town and the water came down the valley covering everything in its path. The devout man climbed to his rooftop and clung there, praying to God for help.

Soon a motor boat came by and a soldier offered him a hand to come aboard. "No, thank you," the man said; "God will save me." As the man could not be coaxed into the boat, the soldiers went on.

Then the water covered the house and the man was forced to swim. Soon another boat came by and the people on board threw him a life preserver. "No, thank you," he called, sputtering a little; "God will save me."

Finally a helicopter hovered above and dropped a line. "No, thank you, God will blub, blub, blub," the man coughed and sputtered as he waved them on and went under, once, twice, three times.

When the man awoke he was in heaven standing before God.

"God, you said you would save me, but you let me die," he complained.

"I tried to save you," God said. "But you refused all my help."

"Not so," the man said.

"Look," God said, "I sent you a motorboat, a life preserver, and a helicopter. If that's not help, I don't know what is!"

Your Story

Explore the story through meditation, visualization, writing, and/or an expressive art form.

Making a Personal Connection with the Story

What meaning does this story have for you?

We all have grown up with certain images of how God's presence in our lives might or should be made known. Do we close ourselves off to all the other ways that it might manifest? How do you think God communicates with or helps you? In what ways do you expect to receive (or not receive) help from God? What is God's role in your life?

Describe any experiences you have had in which you held out, expecting to experience God's presence in your life in a certain way, only to find it in another.

Trying on the Ideas in the Story

Take note in a journal this week of all of the unexpected ways in which you experience love or truth or God. What if an experience of God's love came through in a smile or a piece of music or a traffic jam? Try "what iffing" yourself into all kinds of delightful experiences of God's grace. As the saying goes, "Expect the unexpected."

Sharing the Story with Others

This is a fun story to relate. We all know someone else who would behave like the dear preacher, but this story relates to us as well.

THE RICH MAN'S TREASURES

C h r i s t i a n

And Jesus spoke this parable:

There was a rich man who went away to another country. Before he left, he gave some of his treasures to his three servants: five talents* to the first, two to the second, and one to the third. "Look after it," he said; "trade with it and give it back when I return."

After the master had gone, the first servant went straight to the marketplace. With his five talents he bought and sold all kinds of goods. He worked hard until the five talents his master had given him had been multiplied to ten.

The second servant also took his two talents to the marketplace and with hard work turned his two into four.

The third servant was afraid to do anything with the one talent his master had given him. He dug a hole in the earth and buried it where no one would find it.

After a time the lord returned and wanted to know what his servants had done with his money.

The first servant showed him that he had turned five talents into ten. "Well done," he said. "You have shown that you can be faithful over a few things, I will set you over many things; enter into the joy of your lord."

The second servant also came to him and showed his profit. The lord said unto him as well, "You have shown that you can be faithful over a few things, I will set you over many things; enter into the joy of your lord."

The third servant came forward clutching his one bag of talents and said, "Master, I was afraid to use your treasures. I thought that someone might steal them or cheat me out of them, so I hid them safely in the earth."

The rich man was angry. "I gave you my treasures to use,

36

not to hide," he said. "Give that which I gave you to the man who has ten, he will know what to do with it."

For to those who have, more will be given, and they will have an abundance.

*A talent is a biblical monetary unit that represents a certain weight of silver or gold. One talent was worth over a thousand dollars.

Your Story

Explore the story though meditation, visualization, writing, and/or an expressive art form.

Making a Personal Connection with the Story

What meaning does this story have for you?

Retell the story as if it were your life, using the following questions as guides: What gifts have you been given? How and when have you multiplied them? How and when have you hidden them? What new benefits of freedom or responsibility have been bestowed upon you as a result of using your talents? When and how has your authority or freedom or joy been denied you when you hid your talents like the third servant?

Imagine in detail what your life would be like if you used all the gifts God gave you, as Jesus or the Bal Shem Tov, Mohammed or the Buddha did. What stands in your way? Why do you think we are afraid to run around like ecstatic, lovestruck fools, doing good deeds all day long and having full faith? Gratitude, joy, peace, love, all of these multiply when expressed. Are we afraid that our gifts will be misused or stolen, or that we will spend them all too quickly and then have nothing?

How does this story reflect upon your relationship to money in your daily life?

Trying on the Ideas in the Story

Make a list of your God-given gifts, both those talents given especially to you, such as singing, dancing, or a vivid imagination, and those that all humans would have access to if they really tried, such as a beautiful soul, empathy, compassion, or the ability to express joy. As you go through your week, try to make conscious efforts to dig these up and use them.

Pick a conscious moment each day to let the love that is in your heart multiply and multiply until it pours out of you, overflowing into all that you do and everyone you come into contact with. Write in a journal about how this felt and how you were able to access those gifts so that you can do so more easily in the future.

SHARING THE STORY WITH OTHERS
Would you dare ask others to try to use all of their gifts with you?

eighteen

THE EMPTY CUP

Z e n

One day the Zen master Nan-in had a visit from a foreign scholar of Eastern religions who came to inquire about Zen. Instead of listening to the master, however, the visitor kept talking on and on about his own ideas and all that he knew.

After a while of this talking, Nan-in served tea. He poured the tea into his visitor's cup until it was full, and then he kept on pouring. The tea poured over the side of the cup, filled the saucer, and then spilled over onto the man's pants and the floor.

Finally the visitor could not restrain himself. "Don't you see that it is full?" he said. "You can't get any more in!"

"Just so, " replied Nan-in, stopping at last. "And like this cup, you are filled with your own ideas. How can you except me to give you Zen unless you offer me an empty cup?"

YOUR STORY

Explore the story through meditation, visualization, writing, and/or an expressive art form.

MAKE A PERSONAL CONNECTION WITH THE STORY

Zen teachers refer often to the idea of a "beginner's mind" or an "empty mind" for those wishing to understand Zen. Every spiritual quest requires an inner awareness and quieting of the mind, so that seekers can expand their awareness of what their reality is, and so can learn new ways of being. Almost every spiritual tradition speaks of the importance of silence for opening a space to be with the Creator or with one's own deepest wisdom. Some religions, such as Buddhism, are based on the practice of meditation. Meditation is the act of learning to be attentive to how the mind is responding to external and internal stimuli, and then learning to quiet the mind, returning it to the present moment.

It was the "expert's" ego in this story that kept him from stopping and listening. The ego tries to constantly reinforce who we think we are and what we know, and to prove us better or to chide us for not being so. It is a great risk for the ego to be quiet or uninvolved. The heart, however, knows that great riches are to be found in quiet and stillness. In order to grow to be the loving, peaceful, compassionate beings we long to be, we need to be attentive to our minds and to make room for our hearts to listen and hear. Remember that you cannot change the past or control the future, but you can be master of the present moment.

How is your mind like the scholar's in the story? What activities do you practice in your day to achieve empty-cup stillness and attentiveness?

TRYING ON THE IDEAS IN THE STORY

In the resources section I have listed some excellent books on beginning a meditation practice that is right for you. I suggest that you try a class at first to have the added support of a teacher and the energy of other students. As you go about your week, try to find at least one chunk of time—twenty to thirty minutes in the morning—to sit quietly. Using one of the many techniques suggested, practice mindful awareness and quieting. I suggest that you begin by getting your body stretched out, relaxed, and comfortable.

When you are done with the meditation, take the time to record what happened in your mind. What did you think about, when did you catch yourself, and what helped you return to quiet? The act of writing about it helps you at other times of the day to be more conscious of where your mind is and helps you choose the technique and circumstances that are right for you. Another way to practice is to go for a walk and to try to stay aware of the present moment and what you are experiencing.

Opportunities to practice stillness can also happen at many small moments during the day. As you go through your week, decide on some activities that you do frequently that can be reminders to take some quiet, present-moment, empty-mind time. These are times to come totally into the present and/or to take stock of where your mind has been. Even a few moments can help relieve stress!

You might also notice the impulse to fill up your mind with more information about your spiritual path. There are so many good books out there on spiritual growth that a person could literally be a spiritual book junkie. We can read and read and read to the point where we just can't get any more in. And we may be no closer to inner peace, because we have been reading about the ideas rather than being with them. Try to practice emptying your mind rather than filling it this week. Take a mind-food fast.

Sharing the Stories with Others

For a good way to introduce the idea of quiet times at home or work, see the resources section at the back of the book.

nineteen

MY SINS ARE RUNNING OUT BEHIND ME

Desert Fathers

A brother in Scete happened to commit a fault. The elders assembled and sent for Abbot Moses to join them. He, however, did not want to come. The priests sent him a message, saying, "Come, the community of brethren is waiting for you." So he arose and started off. And taking with him a very old basket full of holes, he filled it with sand and carried it behind him. The elders came out to meet him, and said, "What is this, Father?" The elder replied, "My sins are running out behind me, and I do not see them, and today I come to judge the sins of another!" They, hearing this, said nothing to the brother but pardoned him.

CASTING THE FIRST STONE

Christian

E arly one morning Jesus came to the temple near the Mount of Olives. A crowd of people gathered, and he sat down with them and taught them his messages of peace. The scribes and the Pharisees wanted to test him. So they brought a woman and placed her in the middle of the people, saying to him, "Teacher, this woman has been caught in the act of adultery. The law of Moses commands us to stone such a sinner. What do you say that we should do with her?"

Jesus wrote with his finger in the dirt for a time, and then he stood up and said to them, "Let the one among you who is without sin be the first to throw the stone at her." He went back to his writing, bent over on the ground. But when her accusers heard this they went away one by one, beginning with the eldest, until only Jesus was left in the middle of the crowd with the woman.

Jesus looked up and said, "Woman, where are they? Has no one condemned you?" She said, "No one, my lord." And Jesus said, "Neither do I condemn you; go and do not sin again."

~ ~ ~

YOUR STORY

Explore the stories through meditation, visualization, writing, and/or an expressive art form.

MAKING A PERSONAL CONNECTION WITH THE STORY

Brainstorm a list of times in your life when you have judged others harshly for their actions. Have you ever acted as they did? Do you think you ever could? Think about what really makes a person act in such a way, individually, culturally, politically, economically, and globally. Brainstorm a list of times when you have felt judged harshly. How did it feel?

TRYING ON THE IDEAS IN THE STORY

Because the media is so present in our lives we have many occasions to judge others. These are actually opportunities to practice nonjudgment and compassion toward others, and ultimately toward ourselves.

Notice as you go about your week how often the opportunity arises to judge others because of their actions, appearance, ideas, etc. Step back from judgment and remember your own perfect imperfection. What a comfort to the soul! Imagine yourself to be carrying around that holy basket (pun intended), spilling your imperfections behind you.

SHARING THE STORIES WITH OTHERS

The story of "Casting the First Stone" is one that most Westerners have at least heard and can use as a standard for fair and kind treatment. But how often do we live it? Stories need to be retold again and again to truly enter our daily working consciousness.

Retell this story with modern circumstances whenever you hear negative news stories or encounter judgment in your daily life. This is a good story to have permanently fixed to a public bulletin board!

t w e n t y

THE LION'S WHISKER

E t h i o p i a

Long ago in Ethiopia, a woman married a widower who had a son. Her joy was great when she went to live in the home of her new husband, for she had longed for a child. But the child refused her affections, saying, "You are not my real mother." He refused her cooking, tore her mending, and turned away from her kindness.

After some time, the sorrowing woman decided to seek the help of a wise hermit who lived on the mountain. "Make me a potion," she begged, "so that my stepson will love me as I love him."

"I can make such a potion," he said. "But the ingredients are very difficult to obtain. You must bring me the whisker of a living lion."

The woman went away in great distress but determined not to give up. That night, while her family slept, she crept out of the village to the edge of the desert carrying a bowl of meat. She knew that a great lion lived near some rocks quite a distance away. She walked under the night sky as close to the lion as she dared. Hearing him roar, she dropped the bowl and ran back home. Again the next night, she sneaked from the house with a bowl of meat. She walked further into the desert until she could see the form of the lion on the distant rocks. She set down her bowl and ran home.

Every night she drew closer to the lion before setting down her bowl and fleeing for home. Every night the lion ate her food. Finally one night after many weeks, she placed down her bowl, and stepped back but did not run. She watched the huge cat come slowly forward and eat from the bowl. The following night, she placed down the bowl and did not move away. The lion came slowly forward and began to eat from the bowl. She reached out and stroked his fur. He made happy sounds in his throat. "Thank you, dear friend," she said, and carefully snipped a whisker from his chin. She moved slowly away and then ran all the way to the wise hermit's hut.

"I've brought you the whisker of a living lion," she called, running into his hut. The hermit was sitting before his fire. He took the whisker and examined it closely. "You have indeed," he said, and dropped the whisker into the fire.

"What have you done?" she cried. "That was the whisker for the love potion. You don't know how hard it was to obtain. It has taken me months to win the trust of the lion."

"Can the love and trust of a child be harder to obtain than that of a wild beast?" he asked her. "Go home and think on what you have done."

The woman returned home, and slowly, with love and patience, won the trust and love of her stepson.

~~~~   ~~~~   ~~~~

Your Story

Explore the story through meditation, visualization, writing, and/or an expressive art form.

Making a Personal Connection with the Story

What meaning does this story have for you?

Our modern culture promises us magic potions for nearly everything, from weight loss to love, healing, and wealth. As a result we do not learn to cultivate patience and to chart a slow but sure course toward our goals. Retell this story with yourself as the main character and insert any of your dreams, desires, needs, and goals that seem unattainable.

We all have a child-self that demands to be heard, that is slow to trust, and that needs time to mourn past losses. As any parent knows, a hurting child needs patient care. Are you patient with yourself for the pain and fear that you may feel deep down? Do you have the trust of your own inner child? What could you do to increase this trust?

It is interesting that the woman thought it easier to win the trust of a lion than of another human being. Why do you think this is?

Trying on the Ideas in the Story

As you go through your week, look at the areas in your life in which you desire change. Apply patience to your approach to these changes, and make a list of the small steps you can take to get there one day at a time. Look at the relationships in your life that lack trust. How can you build trust with the help of the ideas in the story? Find opportunities in the day to practice patience—breathing instead of swearing, for instance.

Try to add a new thing that you do this week to win the trust of your inner child, whether it is singing to it, soothing it, doing something creative from its perspective, or praising instead of criticizing it.

Sharing the Story with Others

This story tends to mean something very personal to those who hear it. Depending on your audience you may wish to substitute an estranged husband for the stepchild as in some variants of this tale. See notes for sources of variants.

twenty-one

THE MOST BEAUTIFUL SONG

P y g m y

Once a young Pygmy boy heard the most beautiful song coming from the forest. It was such a beautiful song that he had to go and see who was singing. In the forest he found the bird who was singing this most beautiful song. He brought it back to the camp to feed it. His father was annoyed at having to give food to the bird, but the son pleaded and pleaded and the bird was fed. The next day the bird sang again; it sang the most beautiful song in the forest, and again the boy went to it and brought it back to feed it. This time the father was even more angered, but once again he gave in and fed the bird. The third day the same thing happened. But this time the father took the bird from his son and told his son to go away. When his son had left, the father killed the bird with the most beautiful song, and with the bird he killed the song, and with the song he killed himself and he dropped dead, completely dead, dead forever.

47

~~~   ~~~   ~~~

YOUR STORY

Explore the story through meditation, visualization, writing, and/or an expressive art form.

You may want to work with this story like a dream, honoring its symbolism. Become the characters and tell it as if you were the boy, the bird, the father, a made-up character like a wise, all-seeing grandmother, or even the forest.

MAKING A PERSONAL CONNECTION WITH THE STORY

Retell this story as if it were happening today in your neighborhood. What meaning does it have for you? When the father kills the bird and the song dies, he dies too. What did the song represent? Why did the father die?

What is it that we can't live without even when we are not consciously aware of it? What is it that your soul needs in order to feel happy?

Imagine your life in detail as if your spirit were totally fed. What would feed it?

Tell yourself the stories of times and ways in which you have fully experienced the most beautiful things. Tell about the times when the most beautiful things have been taken from you. What did you keep from those times? What parts of you died that need to be resurrected? What enables you to search for and to find the most beautiful things? How can you heal from their having been killed?

TRYING ON THE IDEAS IN THE STORY

As you go about your week, make a conscious search for the most beautiful thing(s) in your world that will feed your soul. You may find yourself doing some mourning for those things that have been lost. Though this is painful, it will be freeing for you in the long run.

SHARING THE STORY WITH OTHERS

Tell the story and then perhaps share your own modern-day version. Ask your listeners what the most beautiful song would be, or has been, for them.

twenty-two

THE QUAIL'S SONG

Unknown Origin

Once a hunter spied a flock of quail who were feasting in the tall grass at the edge of the forest. With one swift movement he had caught them all in his net. He took the birds home and put them in a cage at the back of his house. The poor birds walked around and around the cage crying and crying. But whenever the man came and tossed in seeds they greedily pecked them up. All but one bird, that is. There was one bird in the cage who refused to eat, and grew thinner and thinner.

At last the day came when the man planned to bring the fattened birds to the market to sell. He looked carefully into the cage inspecting the quality of his flock. When he noticed the thin bird, he opened the cage and took it out to examine it more closely.

"Why, you're nothing but bones," he said. No sooner had he spoken than the bird flew from his hand to the safety of a branch just out of his reach.

The other birds looked at their free sister and cooed sadly. The free bird sang sadly back, "You ate your captor's food and soon you will die. I refused my captor's food, and now I am free."

~ ~ ~

YOUR STORY

Explore the story through meditation, visualization, writing, and/or an expressive art form.

MAKING A PERSONAL CONNECTION WITH THE STORY

When looked at metaphorically, what does this story remind you of in your own life and culture?

We live in a very powerful consumption-oriented culture where we are constantly enticed by other people's images and values. We are tempted to look like other people, be like them, do what they do, and have what they have. The effect is very insidious, and few of us escape unscathed.

Tell the stories of how this has affected your journey toward wholeness and spiritual connection to God and others.

Tell the stories of ways in which you have followed your spirit like the lone quail who attained her freedom.

TRYING ON THE IDEAS IN THE STORY

As you go through the week, be aware of the aspects of your culture that do not support or enhance your development as a free and joy-filled person. Which of these aspects do you feed yourself with anyway? Is there any room for change? Make a list of things that feed your spirit (the arts, outdoor activities, creating community, for example) and see if there is a way to make these more a part of your life, even in small ways.

SHARING THE STORY WITH OTHERS

This story is a good conversation starter.

twenty-three

THE LOST TICKET

Middle East

N asrudin rode the train to work every day. One day, as usual, the train conductor came and asked him for his ticket. He began fumbling around in his coat pockets, and his pant pockets, and then in other people's pockets. He looked in his briefcase, in his bags, and then in other people's bags.

Finally the train conductor said, "Nasrudin, I'm sure you have a ticket. Why don't you look for it in your breast pocket? That is where most men keep it."

"Oh no," said Nasrudin. "I can't look there. Why, if it wasn't there, I would have no hope."

YOUR STORY
Explore the story through meditation, visualization, writing, and/or an expressive art form.

MAKING A PERSONAL CONNECTION WITH THE STORY
Perhaps Nasrudin did not want to look in the right place for his ticket because he was afraid it might really be missing. Write about or describe to a friend what a ticket represents to you symbolically. If the ticket represents a pass to get to something like heaven or enlightenment or a direct relationship with God, what could be more devastating than to find it missing?

Some aspects of our relationship with God—our faith, our hope, or whatever we wish to call it may be so sacred to us that we hide them away and do not even directly touch them ourselves. If we avoid looking deeply and directly for God, it may be because we fear that our illusions will be shattered and that those who told us about God will be wrong.

Where do you think that your key to spiritual awakening is to be found? What dangers does looking for God present for you?

Describe times in which you have felt direct and strong contact with God's grace and love. These "knowing stories" can be lifesavers during discouraging times.

TRYING ON THE IDEAS IN THE STORY

As you go about your week, take time each day to sit quietly and contemplate where you keep your ticket and how you contact it, and celebrate having it available for the journey.

Remember, too, the stories of your direct experiences of God's grace. Keep them in your breast pocket for frequent reference.

SHARING THE STORY WITH OTHERS

With such a short story you may find it effective to repeat the last line. Some people will hear this story and laugh immediately, while others may not quite understand it. Try to allow for a quiet moment following the story, even if you get blank looks. If you think people don't understand, you may want to join them by asking, "What the heck does he mean by that?" and then help them work it out. Even with people who do respond positively, this story requires some quiet thoughtfulness.

twenty-four

A MUSTARD SEED

Buddhist

Long ago in India a young woman had a baby. She loved the child as dearly as life itself. One day the child sickened. Her condition worsened until she died. The mother was beside herself and refused to accept the death of the child. She ran to all the healers in her village, begging them to give her a potion, something to bring the child back to life.

Finally she came before the Buddha. He looked at the dead child and then at the mother. "Yes," he said, "I can make you a potion to bring this child back to life, but the ingredient required to do it is very hard to procure."

"I'll get it," she cried.

"Bring me a mustard seed," he said.

"A mustard seed!" she interrupted. "That will be easy."

"A mustard seed," he went on, "from a house that has not known death."

The woman hurried off to the nearest household. "Please," she begged, "I need a mustard seed for a potion that will bring my baby back to life." The people ran for their mustard seed supply. As they handed it to her she remembered the condition. "Your household has not suffered any deaths, has it?" she asked.

"Oh yes, we lost both of my parents in the last three years," came the reply.

The woman hurried on to the next house. "A mustard seed!" she cried, and it was brought. Then the question, and the answer: "Yes, I lost my husband but three months ago."

To the next house, and the next, and at each house her question was met with the same answer: "Yes, we have known death."

Finally the woman stopped and looked at her child. Her child was dead, like many of the other people who had been lost in her village. The pain was rising in her like a terrible storm, but she knew now that she must let it come. Losing and suffering are as common to people as a mustard seed is to cooking. She returned home and began her grieving.

YOUR STORY

Explore the story through meditation, visualization, writing, and/or an expressive art form.

MAKING A PERSONAL CONNECTION WITH THE STORY

This story reminds us that others suffer as we do, and that our suffering is not a sign that we are inherently bad people. It is part of the human condition.

Western culture seems very uncomfortable with grieving and suffering. We do not understand that grief is a process, that it takes time and hinders one from functioning "normally." Grieving does not fit with our rugged individualist values or with our work-oriented society. And yet we need to grieve at various times in our lives. Our society allows us about six months to grieve when we lose a close relative; perhaps a few weeks when a relationship ends. Rarely do we give ourselves time to grieve over lost opportunities or lost dreams, homes, or careers. And do we ever take time to grieve when we must let go of a part of ourselves so we can expand to our highest potential? Carrying unexpressed grief weighs us down. Grieving frees us from sadness and depression and anger.

Therapist John Lee believes that one of the main losses we need to grieve for is our childhood. Childhood in itself is a spiritual experience, as children are more open to feeling and present-moment experience. What losses will you need to grieve for in your spiritual journey?

Retell this story from your own experience. Attempt to get a mustard seed from a house that has not known job loss, money problems, divorce, depression, anger, problems with intimacy, infertility, addiction, or any kind of suffering.

Tell stories about where your rules for grieving and suffering came from. How did/do your parents grieve?

TRYING ON THE IDEAS IN THE STORY

As you go through your week, notice what rules you have about how you and others can grieve and suffer and grapple with life issues. Rewrite those rules so that you are more accepting of yourself and what you really feel.

Look at the issues that challenge you. How much energy do you spend chastising yourself for having them compared with energy spent actually working with them. Self-acceptance opens the door to healing.

SHARING THE STORY WITH OTHERS

In the first version of this story I heard it was salt that was needed rather than mustard seed. I believe in understanding and celebrating the cultural specifics of a story. I also think the imagery you choose has to make sense to the audience. You may want to start by showing people a mustard seed and asking who has cooked with it or tasted it. If they are not familiar with it, you can ask what seasonings they commonly use in cooking and can substitute one of these instead.

twenty-five

THE CASTLE DOOR

An Original Tale

Once long ago in a distant land, a prince was riding through a deep forest far from his home with his company of soldiers, looking for new lands to conquer. Quite suddenly he came upon a clearing in the trees. There before him stretched a meadow leading to a glorious hill. The meadow and hill were covered with blossoming trees, bushes, and wildflowers. At the top of the hill was a castle that seemed made of pure gold. It sparkled so in the sunlight that the prince was nearly blinded.

Fascinated, the prince signaled to his regiment, and together they rode closer and closer, and up the hill toward the castle. The birds sang sweetly, the perfume of flowers was lovely. As they drew near the castle, he saw that a window opened for a moment in the wall and a face appeared, a face that shone more brilliantly than the sun and yet more gently than any flower. Then it was gone.

Instantly he fell in love.

He knocked upon the castle door.

"Who is there?" came a voice softer than the bluest sky.

"It is I, Prince Rindleheart. I am known throughout the land for my bravery. My armies are the strongest. My castle is but two days' ride from here. May I please come and be with you?"

"There is only room for one of us here" was the reply.

The prince rode away in dejection. He traveled around through seven kingdoms, fighting dragons, escaping from dungeons, taking land. Everywhere he went he was a hero. And yet the praise meant nothing, for everywhere he went he thought only of the shining light of his beloved and of her words, "There is only room for one of us here.

Finally in his desperation he sought the wisdom of a wise woman.

"Perhaps your armies intimidate her," she suggested.

"Of course," he thought.

He returned to the castle alone and knocked upon the door.

"Who is there?" came the sweet voice.

"It is I, the prince, alone," he replied humbly.

"There is only room for one of us here," said the sweet voice.

He went away again, dejected and confused. He roamed the wilderness for some years until he met a famous wizard.

"Perhaps she cannot know you with all of your armor and weaponry," he suggested. "Of course," said the prince.

So he returned and laid down his armor, his shield, and his sword. He walked humbly to the castle door and knocked.

"Who is there?" asked the voice.

"It is I, your humble servant. No soldier, just a man."

"There is only room for one of us here," came the reply.

For seven more years the prince wandered alone in the wilderness, forsaking his kingdom, thinking only of his beloved. He sought wisdom only from the stars in the sky and the wildness inside him.

Finally one day the prince returned to the castle on the hill. He had no armies, no armor, no horse. He walked up the hill, past the bushes heavily laden with the fruit of fall, and knocked upon the door.

"Who is there?" came the sweet voice.

The prince took a breath, and said, "It is thou."

And the door was opened to him.

~ ~ ~

YOUR STORY

Explore the story through meditation, visualization, writing, and/or an expressive art form.

Making a Personal Connection with the Story

What did you like about this story? Was there anything that bothered you? What meaning does this story have for you?

You may wish to see the relationship between the prince and his beloved in the story as a metaphor for how we come to know God in ourselves and in one another. You may wish to see the beloved in the story as God. Following this metaphor, the prince had to relinquish his separate identity in order to fully join with the object of his desire.

When have you known yourself to be one with God? When in your life have you felt separate from God? When have you felt most joined to and most separated from other people? What does it mean to you to say to your creator, "I am thou"?

Imagine this story as if you were the prince and God lived in a golden palace on a hill. How would you gain entrance to dwell within?

Trying on the Ideas in the Story

As you go through your week, contemplate the idea that we are all one with God at our core. How does this fit with your religious or personal beliefs? As mentioned in story 4, *namaste* is a Buddhist salutation that means, roughly, "I acknowledge the God-like place in you, or that place where you and I are one." As you go about your week, try silently greeting each person you meet with "Namaste," and notice how it makes you feel in relation to them.

Sharing the Story with Others

Enjoy the fairy-tale quality of this tale, set the scene and try to enter that faraway place. Make up your own versions, perhaps in a different place and time.

twenty-six

OLD JOE AND THE CARPENTER

North American Traditional

Old Joe lived way out in the countryside all by himself. His best friend was also his closest neighbor. It seemed that they had grown old together. Now that their spouses had passed on, and their children were raised and living lives of their own, all they had left were their farms—and each other.

But for the first time in their long friendship, they'd had a serious disagreement. It was a silly argument over a stray calf that neither one of them really needed. The calf was found on the neighbor's land and he claimed it as his own. Old Joe said, "No, no, now that calf has the same markings as one of my cows, and I say it belongs to me!"

They were stubborn men, and neither would give in. Rather than hit each other, they just stopped talking and stomped off to their respective doors and slammed them shut! Two weeks went by without a word between them.

Come Saturday morning, Old Joe heard a knock on his front door. He wasn't expecting anyone and was surprised to find a young man who called himself a "traveling carpenter" standing on his porch. He had a wooden toolbox at his feet, and there was kindness in his eyes.

"I'm looking for work," he explained. "I'm good with my hands, and if you have a project or two, I'd like to help you out."

Old Joe replied, "Yes, as a matter of fact, I do have a job for you. See that house way over yonder? That's my neighbor's house. You see that creek running along our property line? That creek wasn't there last week. He did that to spite me! He hitched a plow to his tractor and dug that creekbed from the upper pond right down the property line. Then he flooded it!

Now we got this creek to separate us. I'm so darn mad at him! I've got lumber in my barn, boards, posts, everything you'll need to build me a fence—a tall fence—all along that creek. Then I won't have to see his place no more. That'll teach him!"

The carpenter smiled and said, "I'll do a good job for you."

The old man had to go to town for supplies, so he hitched up his wagon and left for the day. The young carpenter carried the lumber from barn to creekside, and started to work. He worked hard and he worked fast. He measured, sawed, and nailed those boards into place all day long without stopping for lunch. With the setting of the sun, he started to put his tools away. He had finished his project.

Old Joe pulled up, his wagon full of supplies. When he saw what the carpenter had built, he couldn't speak. It wasn't a fence. Instead, a beautiful footbridge, with handrails and all, reached from one side of the creek to the other.

Just then, Old Joe's neighbor crossed the bridge, his hand stuck out, and said, "I'm right sorry about our misunderstanding, Joe. The calf is yours. I just want us to go on being good friends."

"You keep the calf, " said Old Joe. "I want us to be friends, too. The bridge was this young fellow's idea. And I'm glad he did it."

The carpenter hoisted his toolbox onto his shoulder and started to leave.

"Wait!" said Joe. "You're a good man. My neighbor and I can keep you busy for weeks."

The carpenter smiled and said," I'd like to stay, but I can't. I have more bridges to build."

And he walked on down the road, whistling a happy tune as he went.

⌒⌒⌒   ⌒⌒⌒   ⌒⌒⌒

YOUR STORY

Explore the story through meditation, visualization, writing, and/or an expressive art form.

MAKING A PERSONAL CONNECTION WITH THE STORY

Brainstorm a list of times in which you have built bridges instead of fences with others. Brainstorm a list of times in which you have built fences instead of bridges. Explore those stories imagining different scenarios.

You may want to look at your intimate relationships separately, because in these we tend to have both bridges and fences. Exploring the fences that we have put up in the face of deep intimacy can be the most profound spiritual work that we do. Learning to truly open our hearts to others is life transforming.

TRYING ON THE IDEAS IN THE STORY

Make a list of people with whom you have built fences. What are your fences made of, and when were they built? Think about what you could do to change the architecture of your relationships. How does it feel to have a fence up with someone? How does it feel to build bridges?

Talk with your intimate partner (or reflect on past relationships) about the fences and bridges in your relationship and how these have changed.

Most people see this as a Christian story and Jesus as the carpenter. Remember that we are all the carpenters of our lives.

SHARING THE STORY WITH OTHERS

Everyone knows someone who is having a feud with someone else. This is a good story to send to feuding relatives or friends.

twenty-seven

THE SWORD OF WOOD

Jewish

Once, on a summer night in Afghanistan, Shah Abbis left his palace dressed as a peasant to enjoy the evening air and to wander through the streets unnoticed. He walked and walked until he reached the poorest section at the edge of town. He soon heard singing coming from a dimly lit cottage. As he peered in the window he saw a man sitting at a table. He was eating and singing and giving thanks to God. The shah was astonished to see such a poor man in such good spirits and so he asked if he might come in as a guest.

After accepting food and drink the shah asked the man how he earned his living. "I am a poor Jew," he said. "I wander the streets and fix shoes, and with whatever I earn I buy enough to sustain myself for one day." "But what will happen to you when you are too old to work?" asked the shah. "Oh, I do not have to worry about that," the man said happily. "God blesses me day by day, I know he will provide."

The shah returned to his palace determined to test the faith of this man. The next day he put out a proclamation forbidding anyone to fix shoes. When the Jew went to work he was astonished to learn of the new law, but he lifted his eyes to heaven and said, "God, the door to my livelihood has been shut. I know that you will help me to find another." He looked around and saw a man carrying water, and he decided that he too would become a water carrier. He carried water to and from the town well, selling just enough to buy food for himself for one day.

The shah again disguised himself and returned to the man's house. He was surprised to find the man again singing and eating. "How are you?" he asked upon entering. "I heard of the law and had to see how you had survived the day." "God did not abandon me today," the Jew answered happily. "The shah closed one door, but God opened another to take its place. I am now a water carrier."

The shah took his leave again and the next day issued a proclamation that no one was to carry water for pay. Again the Jew spoke to God, and this time he saw that men were going into the forest to cut trees to sell for firewood. This he also did, making just enough to buy food for one day.

Again the shah came in disguise and learned of the man's continued faith and good fortune. The next day he issued a command that his soldiers stop all the woodcutters coming from the forests and bring them to the palace to work. He dressed them all as guards and gave them swords. He told them that they would not be paid until the end of the month. The peasant was perplexed indeed, for he had no money for that evening, let alone another month. But he told God that he trusted him to provide.

On the way home, while examining his sword and sheath, he had a clever idea. He would make a sword of the same size out of wood and then sell the shah's sword. When it was done, the money he got for the metal was enough to live on until the end of the month.

The shah was much surprised to find the peasant singing and eating that night. When he heard the Jew's story about the sword, he asked him, what he would do if the shah found out what he had done. "Oh, I do not worry about such things," the Jew replied. "God blesses me day by day, he will not abandon me, my confidence in him is strong."

The next day the shah ordered the guards to report to the center of the city where there was to be an execution of a man who had stolen from the royal garden. All the townspeople came. The shah ordered his officer to call the Jew to come forth to cut off the man's head. "Do not ask this of me," the Jew cried. "I have never even killed a fly." The officer said that it was the order of the shah and he must obey or risk his own life.

The Jew asked for a few minutes to pray to God. Then he stood up in front of all of the townspeople and said out loud, "God, you know that I have never killed anyone in my whole life. Please, God, if this man is guilty, let my sword be so sharp as to kill him in a single blow. But if he is not guilty, let my sword turn to wood, as a sign of his innocence." With all eyes on him, he reached for his sword, pulled it out of its sheath, and held it high. The crowd gasped, then clapped and cheered when they saw the wooden sword, for they assumed a miracle had taken place.

The shah was delighted when he saw the wisdom of the Jew. He called him near. He told him that he had been the visitor those four preceding nights. "And now," he said, "I hope that you will come and stay with me in my palace and be my adviser, for I see that you are a man of wisdom and unwavering faith, and I have much to learn from you."

So the Jew went to live in the palace with the shah. If you went by there in the evenings, you would hear them singing.

YOUR STORY

Explore the story through meditation, visualization, writing, and/or an expressive art form.

MAKING A PERSONAL CONNECTION WITH THE STORY

The poor Jew in this story lived in constant faith and gratitude, thinking only of meeting his needs day by day rather than worrying out into the future. He lived in a state of love rather than fear. Imagine what your life would be like if you practiced these ideas.

Retell the story as if you were the poor Jew, putting it in the context of your own life history. Describe times in your life when you didn't know what to do next, or had nothing left to fall back on, and how help came to you.

What do you believe about how well you will be helped in difficult times? What do you see as God's role in helping you to survive and fulfill your dreams?

TRYING ON THE IDEAS IN THE STORY

Try walking around in the shoes of the poor Jew for a week. When you do this, you might like to create a mantra or affirmation for yourself, such as "God blesses me, day by day," that you say whenever a worry or fear comes into your mind.

The poet William Blake said, "Gratitude is heaven itself." Cultivating gratitude has its own rewards. One way to cultivate a grateful heart is to keep a "gratitude journal." Every night before you go to sleep, write about the things that you feel grateful for, both the major players in your life, and the day-to-day lessons and experiences. You will be surprised how quickly you come to realize the blessings in every circumstance, even the painful and awkward ones!

SHARING THE STORY WITH OTHERS

This is a wonderful story to tell at family or other group gatherings. It is a bit longer than some of the others, but if you follow the steps in learning a story listed in the introduction you will have no trouble remembering the sequence of events and telling it in your own words.

twenty-eight

WATER NOT WINE

Africa and China

Once upon a time, the eldest and richest man in a village decided that it would be a good idea to give a feast for all of the townspeople at the start of the new year. He called the council of ten elders together to plan the event. "I will provide the feast," he said, "if you will each bring a jug of wine."

"Of course, of course," they all agreed.

But as soon as they had parted, the youngest of the group was already cursing himself for having agreed to part with one whole jug of wine. He did not have much wine in his stores, and he did not want to spend money either. "There must be another way," he told his wife. And he sat down to think.

After a while a smile crossed his face. "The other nine elders will pour their wine into the common pot. Could one jug of water spoil so much wine?"

"Hardly so, my clever husband," she answered.

And so it was that on the day of the feast this man put on his finest robes, filled his jug with fresh water from the well, and went to the party. On his way he met up with the other elders. They were greeted at the party by the sounds of music playing, and the delicious smells of food cooking. The host motioned for the elders to pour their jugs of wine into a great clay pot in the courtyard.

First there was dancing and entertainment. Then the bell was rung and the guests were seated.

The elders sat together at the head table. The host ordered his servants to fill everyone's cups with the wine. Each of the elders waited patiently for the last guest to be served. They were anxious to taste the fine, refreshing wine.

The host gave the signal and the guests put their cups to their lips. They sipped, and sipped again. But what they tasted was not wine but water, for each of them had thought, "One jug of water cannot spoil a great pot of wine." Each of them had filled his jug at the well.

They looked at each other sheepishly, avoiding the eyes of the host, and then continued to drink as if it were the finest wine their lips had ever tasted.

That day a new saying arose among the people of the village, a saying that spread around the world: "If you wish to take wine, you must give it also."

~ ~ ~

Your Story
Explore the story through meditation, visualization, writing, and/or an expressive art form.

Making a Personal Connection with the Story
Fear of lack is so pervasive in our time that many hoard their goods while millions of people around the world are starving or hungry. Meanwhile there would be enough to go around if we only shared.

Brainstorm a list of times when you have given your wine. Tell these stories.

Brainstorm a list of times in which you have given water instead of wine, or when those around you seem to have done so. Tell these stories.

Trying on the Ideas in the Story
As you go about your week, notice the opportunities to give water or wine and the choices you make. Make a conscious choice to give wine to some of the projects or daily encounters that you are involved in.

Sharing the Story with Others
This is a fun story to modernize, setting it in your own town, workplace or home. Kids can relate to it when it is set in their school—perhaps a special event to which they were all supposed to bring lemonade.

twenty-nine

THE FATHER, THE SON,
AND THE DONKEY

Buddhist and Aesop

One day a farmer decided that his donkey was fat enough to take to market to sell. He called to his son and told him to bring two poles. "We will carry our donkey to market on these two poles so that she will not get too thin from walking the long distance," he said.

So they tied the donkey to the poles, hoisted the poles upon their shoulders, and headed down the road to market. The donkey hung upside down between them braying and heehawing in dismay.

Soon they came by a group of people in the road. The people saw them and began to laugh. "Look at you stupid fellows carrying a donkey like it was a pig. That donkey should be carrying you! Why don't you get on its back and ride it?"

When the farmer and his son heard the laughter and jeering they were very embarrassed. When the people had gone, they stopped. The farmer said, "I guess we must look rather strange carrying a donkey. Perhaps we should put her down and ride upon her, as they suggested. But, really, she is too small for both of us to ride her. Suppose you ride, since you are smaller, and I will walk in front carrying the packs."

The son agreed, so they untied the donkey and the son got up on her, and they began again down the road.

They had gotten nearly to the river when again they came upon a group of people. This time they called out to the son, "Hey, boy, what kind of a son are you riding in comfort while your poor old father must walk carrying the bags? You should be ashamed of yourself."

The red-faced son dismounted. "Perhaps you should ride, father, and I will carry the pack," the son suggested. "Yes, son," the farmer agreed. "Perhaps that will be the best."

So the father got up on the donkey and the son walked in front with the pack.

They crossed the river and entered the village where the market was. Soon they came upon a group of young women at the side of the road. "Look at that handsome young man walking like a servant while the old goat rides like a prince. You should ride, handsome boy, and the old man should walk."

The boy turned to his father. "Father, have we made a mistake again?" he asked. "Yes, son," replied the father. "It seems we have made several mistakes today. First we carried the donkey and people said it was wrong, then you rode and people said it was wrong, then I rode and people said it was wrong. Perhaps we should both ride together."

"Splendid," said the boy. So they both got up on the donkey and continued on their way. When they reached the marketplace a crowd of people gathered there turned and stared at them. "How could you be so cruel?" they called out. "That donkey is barely old enough for one rider, and yet you have put two on her. That donkey is so little, you should be carrying her! Shame, shame," the people cried out louder and louder.

The farmer and his son got off at once, but the crowd was so loud that it frightened the poor donkey, who bucked and kicked itself free and ran off, never to be seen again.

❦   ❦   ❦

YOUR STORY
Explore the story through meditation, visualization, writing, and/or an expressive art form.

MAKING A PERSONAL CONNECTION WITH THE STORY
It has been said that the surest way to fail is to try to please everybody.

The old man and his son valued the opinions of others more than their own. Make a list of times when you have been ruled by the impressions and opinions (real or construed) of others. Tell these stories.

Imagine fully living your highest vision. Whose judgments would you have to face to make these changes in your life? Who and what are standing in your way? Tell this story with a positive outcome.

Do you have certain people who stand in judgment in your mind? Are there different people who judge over different areas; work, relationships, body image, political activism?

How willing are you to talk about or practice your spirituality publicly? Does this have to do with your perception of how others will judge you?

How well do you hear your own inner voice? What would it mean to listen to that voice above all others?

TRYING ON THE IDEAS IN THE STORY

As you go about your week, notice when you are judging yourself. Try to identify whose voices (e.g., mother's, father's, teacher's, friend's) are behind the shaming, judging, and criticizing of yourself. Notice when you are swayed by the opinions of others and when you let your own inner wisdom be your guide. When you have decisions to make, try going to a quiet place inside and asking yourself for answers before deciding.

SHARING THE STORY WITH OTHERS

This is a fun story to relate. Let yourself become the characters (we carry them all inside us). Try telling this story from the viewpoint of the donkey, the son, or the father. Make up a modern-day version.

t h i r t y

THE TREE OF SORROWS

J e w i s h

In a small village in Poland there lived a wise rabbi. His followers loved him and came often to tell him of their woes. After a while the rabbi grew tired of hearing each one claim that their lot in life was so much more difficult to bear than their neighbor's. They were constantly asking, "Why doesn't he have to suffer as I do? Why doesn't she have a nagging husband, or why doesn't he have a lazy wife? Why doesn't she have back trouble, and why don't his children still live at home contributing nothing to the family's income?" On and on it went until the rabbi came up with a plan.

He sent out word that there was to be a new holiday celebrated. "Bring your sorrows and troubles," he announced. "Bring them in a bag with your name on it and hang the bag from the great tree in the center of the village. All will be allowed to exchange troubles and to go home with those of your neighbor rather than your own."

The villagers were excited, imagining how much easier their lives would be from that day on. When the day came, they assembled beneath the tree with bags in hand. With bits of rope they tied their bags to the low branches of the tree so that all might inspect them. "Now," said the rabbi in a very official voice, "if you will all move about inspecting the bags, you may choose someone else's troubles to take home, thus freeing yourselves from your own."

The villagers rushed at the tree and began grabbing at and peering into bags, one after the other, around and around, around and around the tree . . .

Finally, quite tired out and feeling both foolish and wiser, they each sought out their own bags and walked home. The rabbi smiled. It was just as he had hoped. The villagers had seen the sorrows of others as they really were, and had decided to stick with their own lots in life because, at least, they were familiar.

YOUR STORY
Explore the story through meditation, visualization, writing, and/or an expressive art form.

MAKING A PERSONAL CONNECTION WITH THE STORY
Who has not imagined that their own problems are worse than those of others? Imagine that this story took place today in your community. Walk around the tree and look into other people's bags. Would your story end the way the folktale does?

What about blessings? Imagine that you put your blessings in a bag. What would the bag contain? Would you trade them for someone else's?

TRYING ON THE IDEAS IN THE STORY
As you go about your week, notice when you compare yourself with another and wish for their good fortune. Imagine that you could switch. Would you still want to?

SHARING THE STORY WITH OTHERS
What a hilarious play this would make! See also "A Mustard Seed" (story 24).

thirty-one

LOVE DOGS

Jelaluddin Rumi

One night a man was crying,
Allah! Allah!
His lips grew sweet with the praising,
until a cynic said,
"So I have heard you calling out,
but have you ever gotten any response?"

The man had no answer to that.
He quit praying and fell into a confused sleep.

He dreamed he saw Khidr, the guide of souls,
in a thick green foliage.
"Why did you stop praising?"
"Because I've never heard anything back."
"This longing you express is the return message."

The grief you cry out from
draws you toward union.

Your pure sadness
that wants help
is the secret cup.

Listen to the moan of a dog for its master.
That whining is the connection.

There are love dogs
no one knows the names of.
Give your life to be one of them.

⌒ ⌒ ⌒

Your Story

Explore the story through meditation, visualization, writing, and/or an expressive art form.

Making a Personal Connection with the Story

This is a difficult message to swallow—our longing is the connection—and yet at the same time it is very sweet.

Describe times in which you have longed for that which is God-like. How did you "call out"? Describe the sense of connection you felt in your longing.

Trying on the Ideas in the Story

There are many ways to cry out to the presence that we desire union with. Artists do it in a myriad of ways. Religions prescribe specific ways of doing it. Many people do it without even feeling "religious."

As you go about the week, experiment with different ways of connecting to the presence through longing—singing, praying silently or out loud, dancing, making music, painting, writing, crying into the wind . . . See how your moan for your master can be the connection, and how the longing that you cry out from is the secret cup. Be a love dog.

Sharing the story with others

This is a good one to copy and send around for quiet contemplation. It may be better to read this aloud than to try to tell it from memory because its particular wording is so beautiful.

THE TORN CLOAK

Desert Fathers

An elder was asked by a certain soldier if God would forgive a sinner. And he said to him, "Tell me, beloved, if your cloak is torn, will you throw it away?" The soldier replied and said, "No, I will mend it and put it back on." The elder said to him, "If you take such care of your cloak, will God not be merciful to His own image?"

SIN

Anthony de Mello, S.F. (adapted)

It is said that God up in heaven holds each one of us by a string. When we sin, we are in essence cutting the string; the connection between ourselves and God, ourselves and what we know, ourselves and others. When we cut the string and realize what we have done, we ask for God's help or forgiveness, and she ties the string again, making a knot—and thereby bringing us closer. Again and again we cut the string—and again and again our Creator reties it. With each knot our strings become shorter and shorter, and we are drawn closer and closer to God.

~~~ ~~~ ~~~

YOUR STORY
Explore the stories through meditation, visualization, writing, and/or an expressive form.

Making a Personal Connection with the Stories

These stories deal with the concept of sin. They describe sin as a separation or tearing of the connection between ourselves and God. What does the word sin mean to you? To get a handle on this you might think of times when you considered yourself to have sinned. Tell or write the stories of how your definition of sin was formed as a child and if it has changed over time.

The stories also talk about the forgiving nature of God. Do you agree with this description of the Creator? It has been suggested that we can imagine God's love as unconditional only to the extent that we felt similar love from our parents. This is probably not entirely true. Many of us rise above our childhood experiences with the help of our spiritual beliefs. Take some time to write or talk about God's conditional or unconditional love. Write about or share the nature of your parents' love.

When in your life have you felt as if you were being mended by God? When have you felt drawn closer to God through sin? What experiences in life have drawn you closer to God?

The stories offer an image of a torn cloak mended and cut string knotted. What metaphors would you create to describe your times of connection and disconnection to God?

Trying on the Ideas in the Stories

As you go through your week, observe how conditional or unconditional your love is for yourself and for others. When relations with yourself or others strain or break, hold the image of mending them as you would your dearest garment, and retie the string.

Imagine that there is a string between you and God. Use it as a way to communicate as you go through your week.

Sharing the Stories with Others

These will fit in your pocket for the right moment. They are a great way to open dialogue.

thirty-three

DESCENT INTO THE MAELSTROM

Edgar Allan Poe (adapted)

The fishing between the islands offshore of one particular spot on the Norwegian coastline was especially good, but of all the fishermen in the area, only two brothers ever dared to fish there. For twice every day between the islands and the shore, a horrendous whirlpool some half-mile in diameter would form and suck down every object or living thing that came within several miles of it. People called it "The Great Maelstrom."

One day these two brothers, sure of perfect weather, set sail to the islands, enjoyed a marvelous catch, and then headed home well before the pool was to form. Suddenly, however, the winds changed, stranding them. Before they could row back to the islands a hurricane wind was upon them, tossing them wildly about and snapping their mainsail's mast.

The younger brother clung to a ring bolt at the front of the boat and the elder brother grabbed an empty barrel that was lashed to the back. They rode this way for some time. Suddenly, as they crested a wave, they saw that their tiny boat was heading straight toward the forming pool. In his terror the elder brother at the back lunged and forced the ring bolt from his brother's hand. This brother did not contest the other's fear but went to the back and held on to the water cask.

Finally the inevitable moment came and the tiny ship careened into the whirlpool. The younger brother closed his eyes, said a prayer, and waited for certain death. After a moment however, when death hadn't come, he opened his eyes to find that the boat had not fallen into the abyss but was hanging on the edge of the pool, riding around and around, going slowly down.

Looking up at the sides of the pool and knowing now that death was unavoidable, his fear all but left him. He began to notice with fascination that there were many other objects in the pool—trees, boats, furniture. He began to take interest in the differing speeds with which the objects fell and finally plunged into the swirl. As he watched, a stunning realization was forming in his mind: the lighter, cylindrical objects fell more slowly, while the heavier objects dropped more quickly into the abyss.

This realization set his heart to pounding and his mind to racing. He knew that their only hope of surviving was to lash themselves to the empty water cask and throw themselves out of the boat. He motioned to his brother and, using hand signals, explained his plan. But his brother dropped his head and gripped the ring ever harder, choosing the familiarity of his boat over the uncertainty of the waters. At last, resigning him to his fate, the younger brother cut free the water cask, lashed himself to it, and jumped into the cold black wall of the pool.

It was just as he had hoped. His barrel sank but little more while the small boat went steadily down and finally hurtled his poor brother to his death. Soon the pool began to change. The whirl began to slow and the bottom to rise up. It wasn't long before he found himself again on the surface of the water with the shores of his home in sight.

He was picked up early the next morning by fishermen from his own village. But the fishermen knew him not. For when he had left that morning, his hair had been as black as a raven. When they hauled him in, it was as white as snow.

~ ~ ~

Your Story

Explore the story through meditation, visualization, writing, and/or an expressive art form.

Making a Personal Connection with the Story

The surviving brother in this story knew that he had to let go of his familiar boat and jump into the dark waters of the sea in order to save his life. The other brother preferred to hold on to the safety of the known and thus went down with his ship. Once the surviving brother accepted his circumstances, he was able to be present in the pool and to make the observations that saved him.

The process of evolving and transforming our lives is a lot like trying to save our lives. We need to let go of old familiar habits and aspects of our self in order to let healthier, higher aspects prevail. This process is not an easy on. Identity changes involve fear of the unknown and a temporary disorganization of self. The surviving brother's hair color changes; we too will experience changes and losses.

What stories can you tell about letting go of the familiar for something more life-affirming? Have you altered your ways of relating to your family members, your career choices, or aspects of your identity that no longer serve you? What changes are still to come? How can you apply the metaphors in this story to your process of spiritual growth?

Trying on the Ideas in the Story

As you go about your week, notice what behaviors and habits feel "old and familiar" but not particularly life-affirming. The light, cylindrical water cask allowed the brother to stay afloat. Imagine that you have those qualities of lightness this week and see how you rise above the whirlpool of stress and pain. Explore what your "water cask" might be and test the waters.

Sharing the Story with Others

If this story intrigues you, it is well worth finding the full version and touching Poe's soul through his rich language and imagery. I would suggest reading the full version to others. My shorter version can be learned for telling. This is one of very few stories I tell professionally in which I have chosen to memorize a good bit of the original language. It's worth the effort!

thirty-four

THE DIFFERENCE BETWEEN
HEAVEN AND HELL

Japan

Long ago in Japan an old woman wanted to see for herself the difference between heaven and hell. The monks in the temple agreed to grant her request. "First you shall see hell," they said as they put a blindfold over her eyes.

When the blindfold was removed the old woman stood at the entrance to a great hall. The hall was filled with round tables each piled high with the most delicious feast—meats, vegetables, fruits of every kind, and desserts to make your mouth water. The old woman noticed that there were people seated just out of arm's reach of the tables. Their bodies were thin and their pale faces convulsed with frustration. They held chopsticks almost three feet long. With the chopsticks they could reach the food, but they could not get the food back into their mouths. As the old woman watched, a hungry, angry sound rose into the air. "Enough," she said. "Let me see heaven."

When the blindfold was removed the second time, the old woman rubbed her eyes. For there she stood again at the entrance to a great hall with tables piled high with the same sumptuous feast. Again she saw the people sitting just out of arm's reach of the food with those long chopsticks.

But the people in heaven were plump and rosy-cheeked, and as she watched, the musical sound of laughter filled the air. And then the old woman laughed, for now she understood the difference. The people in heaven were using those three-feet-long chopsticks to feed each other.

Your Story

Explore the story through meditation, visualization, writing, and/or an expressive art form.

Making a Personal Connection with the Story

What does this story mean to you? What is the difference between heaven and hell? How would you retell this story using your own imagery? What times in your life have felt like "hell" and what times like "heaven"?

In heaven each person fed others but was also fed by others. Tell the stories of how you feed others. Tell the stories of how others feed you. Do you allow yourself to be fed by others?

The people in both heaven and hell were handicapped in that they could not feed themselves directly. What are your handicaps, and how could you let others feed you more?

Trying on the Ideas in the Story

As you go through the week, notice when you focus on "feeding" yourself, "feeding" others, being "fed" by others, and sharing with others. Try to create an opportunity for mutual feeding this week—for example, a time of trading stories, sharing a difficult task, or asking for help.

Sharing the Story with Others

This story has immediate applications anywhere that two or more are gathered.

thirty-five

ONLY A VISITOR

Hasidic

Once some tourists from the United States were visiting Poland. They had heard about the famous Polish rabbi Hafez Hayyim and managed to receive an invitation to visit him in his home.

When the tourists arrived, they were surprised to see that the rabbi's home was only one simple room filled with books. His only furniture was a table and a bench.

"Rabbi, where is your furniture?" they asked.

"Where is yours?" replied the rabbi.

"But we are only visitors here," answered the tourists.

"So am I," said the rabbi.

❧   ❧   ❧

YOUR STORY

Explore the story through meditation, visualization, writing, and/or an expressive art form.

MAKING A PERSONAL CONNECTION WITH THE STORY

What does the rabbi's reply mean to you? What do you believe about the soul, afterlife, and/or reincarnation?

Imagine that you are "only a visitor" here on earth. How does that affect your perspective on what is important in your life's journey? With eyes closed, imagine your soul's evolutionary journey from its beginning to the present. You may wish to write this story down or share it with others.

For every traveler there is a place called "home." Describe your spiritual home using some expressive form.

Perhaps the story made you reflect on how material wealth and possessions dominate our lives and thoughts. For many people the story supplies a much-needed sense of relief. As if to say, "Oh, whew, I don't have to spend so much energy trying to get more money and more things!"

Imagine your life if lived sparsely like Rabbi Hayyim's.

Trying on the Ideas in the Story

Reminding ourselves that we are only souls visiting earth can be very helpful for putting things in perspective. It allows us to surface and take a breath of cosmic air before facing our lives again.

As you go about your week, try putting up signs in your car or at home or work saying "visitor" to remind you to think of your life in the larger context of your soul's journey.

Sharing the Story with Others

It is fascinating to hear other people's ideas about what is important in life.

thirty-six

THE MESSIAH IS AMONG US

Unknown Origin

Once there was a monastery that had fallen upon hard times. Some of the younger monks had left in dissatisfaction, and no new men were joining. There were but a handful of monks and their leader, the abbot, remaining. They began fighting among themselves, each blaming the hard times on the faults and failings of the other.

One day a traveling rabbi stopped at the monastery for a night's rest. He ate, and prayed alongside the other monks. The next day, as the rabbi prepared to continue on his journey, the abbot drew him aside. He told him of the problems of the monastery and asked him for his observations and for some advice to share with the other monks.

Upon hearing the abbot's woes, the rabbi was quiet for some time.

"Cannot you give me some advice to help my monastery to thrive again?" the abbot begged.

"Your monks will not listen to my advice," the rabbi replied. "But perhaps they would benefit from an observation. The Messiah dwells among you here at the monastery."

"One of us?" asked the abbot astonished. "Which one?"

"Oh, that I cannot say," he answered. "Share this with your brothers, and in time it shall be revealed to you."

The abbot thanked him and sent him on his way. He then gathered the monks together, who listened in amazement to the news.

"One of us! But who?" each one asked out loud. Then to themselves they wondered, "It couldn't be Brother Robert—or could it?"

"Surely not Brother Henry, but there are times when . . .

"Not the youngest, well, maybe . . ."

"The abbot himself?"

"Could it be me?"

Soon things began to change at the monastery as each began to see the Messiah in the other and to hear the Messiah's words in each word spoken.

Soon people began to wander back to the monastery, and in time new men joined and the monastery thrived.

Your Story

Explore the story through meditation, visualization, writing, and/or an expressive art form.

Making a Personal Connection with the Story

Why do we treat one another so differently than we would treat a Messiah? Make a modern-day version of this story in which you learn that the Messiah is living in your community. What changes? What if the Messiah were you?

Trying on the Ideas in the Story

Imagine this week that the Messiah is now on earth and walking among us. It could be anyone in your family, your workplace, your town. With this is mind, how do you see people, treat people, listen to and learn from people?

Try treating yourself as if you were the Messiah. Pick one person that you interact with frequently. Without telling them, imagine that they are the Messiah and see how it changes your interactions with them for a day. Try treating others in the same way.

Sharing the Story with Others

This story is perfect for boosting morale and nurturing your environment. Try retelling a modern-day version as well.

thirty-seven

SURVIVAL

Anthony de Mello, S.J.

Each day the disciple would ask the same question: "How shall I find God?"

And each day he would get the same mysterious answer: "Through desire."

"But I desire God with all my heart, don't I? Then why have I not found him?"

One day the master happened to be bathing in the river with the disciple. He pushed the man's head underwater and held it there while the poor fellow struggled desperately to break loose.

The next day it was the master who began the conversation. "Why did you struggle so when I held your head under water?"

"Because I was gasping for air."

"When you are given the grace to gasp for God the way you gasped for air, you will have found him."

YOUR STORY

Explore the story through meditation, visualization, writing, and/or an expressive art form.

MAKING A PERSONAL CONNECTION WITH THE STORY

In the story the monk told the student that if he truly wanted to know God, he must gasp for God the same way he gasped for air. Perhaps this is why we tend to find God when we need God most. Describe times in your life when necessity has made you "gasp" for God.

What brings you closer to knowing God? Imagine having passion or desire that is strong enough to bring you to God. What would this look like?

TRYING ON THE IDEAS IN THE STORY

Many of us desire to know God and that which is God-like in ourselves and others. This is at the top of our list of things that we want to accomplish in our lifetime. With all the demands that life makes of us, however, we do not put it on the short list until we have a crisis and need to lean on God.

Make a list of your spiritual goals. Prioritize it by including the time lengths for achievement: immediate, within the year, one year, two, five, ten, and twenty, etc. What can you make happen this week?

This week practice gasping for God in your own way. How does it feel? What way would feel genuine?

SHARING THE STORY WITH OTHERS

This story is a great conversation starter. Follow it with a personal anecdote if possible, and help others share their stories of times when they gasped for God because of necessity or longing.

See also the poem/story "Love Dogs" (story 31).

thirty-eight

THE WISDOM OF ALLAH

Middle East

One day, when Nasrudin the Hodja was working in his garden, he became very warm. He sat down in the shade of a walnut tree, and, making sure that no one was about, he slipped off his turban to cool his bald head. As he relaxed, he meditated upon the beauty of nature and the great wisdom of Allah.

Observing a fine pumpkin in the garden, he smiled to himself. "Allah, your ways are great indeed," he mused out loud, "but there are a few things that I would have done differently were I in charge. See the proud pumpkin growing on a spindly little vine, and then consider the walnut, a tiny, inconsequential nut upon a great and lordly tree. Well, if I had been planning things, I would have reversed it. I'd have hung those pumpkins in all of their glory from this magnificent tree, and let the tiny walnuts cling to the spindly pumpkin vine on the ground." So musing, he closed his eyes to dream of the other things he might do differently. A gentle breeze stirred the branches above him.

Suddenly a walnut fell from the tree and landed with a thud on the top of the Hodja's bald head. As the pain spread, he rubbed the lump that had begun to swell on his scalp. Then an understanding smile spread over his face. He bowed down toward Mecca.

"Oh, Allah," he murmured, "forgive me. Thy wisdom is great indeed. Suppose I had been arranging matters? I should just now have been hit upon the head by a pumpkin. Ah, Allah, great indeed is thy wisdom."

Your Story

Explore the story through meditation, visualization, writing, and/or an expressive art form.

Making a Personal Connection with the Story

There are so many things in life that we cannot understand. Why did the Creator make these choices, allow this to happen, or that? Why is there so much suffering in the world? Have you ever cursed the heavens in utter dumbfoundedness? Who has the answers?

Retell the story with yourself as Nasrudin. Have you ever thought that you could make a better world? Can you think of examples of things you would change if you could? Trying to think of the consequences to their end point is quite a challenge. What would you change about life if you had the Creator's power? What implications would that have for the world? What does it mean to you to trust in the Creator's way? When have you had to submit or surrender to the Creator's way?

Trying on the Ideas in the Story

As you go about your week, notice things and events in your world that you do not understand and that you wish were different. Decide what is in your power to change and what must be accepted with grace and serenity.

Reinhold Niebuhr's Serenity Prayer says:

> *God, give us*
> *grace to accept with serenity the things that cannot be changed,*
> *courage to change the things that should be changed,*
> *and the wisdom to distinguish the one from the other.*

If you like this prayer you might consult it as you meet with various circumstances throughout your week. You might also try saying, "Ah, the wisdom of . . ." to circumstances that you do not understand.

Sharing the Story with Others

See the other Nasrudin stories (5, 23, 38, and 44) and the Zen story (13).

thirty-nine

BLIND MAN PRAYING AT THE WALL

Rabbi Abraham Twerski

I once saw a blind man being led to the wall in Jerusalem. He felt the stones with his fingertips, applied a gentle kiss to those sacred stones, and began speaking to God. Although he spoke very rapidly, I could catch some of the words. He was relating to God various things that had happened to him that day and some of his requests.

At one point he stopped abruptly. "Oh, I'm sorry," he said. "I already told you that yesterday."

The sincerity of the man's prayer was electrifying. He had no doubt whatever that what he had said yesterday had been heard.

90

"I AM PRAYER"

Hasidic

This is what Rabbi Bunham said concerning the verse in the Psalm: "And I am prayer."

"It is as if a poor man, who has not eaten in three days and whose clothes are in rags, should appear before the king. Is there any need for him to say what he wants? This is how David faced God; he *was* prayer."

~~~ ~~~ ~~~

YOUR STORY

Explore the stories through meditation, visualization, writing, and/or an expressive art form.

MAKING A PERSONAL CONNECTION WITH THE STORIES

These stories have some similarities and some differences. What appealed to you, and what didn't? Look at those things that made you uncomfortable and see what that tells you about your belief in and use of prayer.

How do you pray? Go back to various times in which you remember praying, times when you were in crisis and needed help right away, times when someone else needed help and you were praying for them, times when you were trying to make a connection to God.

Remember the stories regarding how you were taught (or not taught) to pray. What prayers were prominent in your home or place of worship? Did you understand what they meant? Did you think that God would answer your prayers? If so, what did you think you had to do for God to answer your prayers or to even hear them?

Do you believe that God hears your prayers? Do you believe that God knows your prayer even before you ask? Do you repeat your prayers? If so, why?

If you *are* prayer, then how should you pray?

TRYING ON THE IDEAS IN THE STORIES

As you go about your week, try having faith that the one that created you and everything in the universe knows you, and what you are facing. Walk around this week *being* prayer. How do you feel?

SHARING THE STORIES WITH OTHERS

It is a very personal thing to talk about how you pray. Choose your confidants wisely.

f o r t y

THE WILD STRAWBERRY

Z e n

The Buddha told this parable:

A man traveling through the mountains suddenly found himself being chased by a huge hungry tiger. He ran and ran until he came to the edge of a cliff. There, with nowhere else to go, he caught hold of a thick vine and swung himself over the edge.

Above him the tiger growled. Below him he heard a sound, and looked down to see another tiger waiting for him at the bottom of the vine.

Two mice, a white mouse and a black mouse, scrambled out from the cliffside and began to gnaw at the vine. The traveler could see they were quickly eating through it. Then in front of him on the cliff side a delicious smell caught his attention. Ah, a luscious wild strawberry! Holding onto the vine with one hand, he reached and picked the berry with the other.

How delicious!

~ ~ ~

YOUR STORY
Explore the story through meditation, visualization, writing, and/or an expressive art form.

MAKING A PERSONAL CONNECTION WITH THE STORY
There is a Hasidic story in which the rabbi asks his students what they would do if they had only one hour to live. Each gave good answers about studying the Torah and other holy works. But the best answer was given by a student who said that he would do what he had been doing, for all of life is sacred.

Being able to fully experience the present moment puts fears of the future and regrets of the past away. It allows us to realize that there is a core to our being that is okay no matter what is going on around us. Appreciating the present moment lets us touch the sweetness, the holiness in all of life.

The present moment is the only one we will ever have control over. Some say that the present moment is where God lives.

Describe a time when you felt completely in the moment. Was it when you walked in quiet natural surroundings? While taking a bath or in meditation? While exercising? Making love?

TRYING ON THE IDEAS IN THE STORY

Stop at various points during your day and just be in the moment. Be aware of doing each activity not to get it done, but to enjoy the doing.

You might try setting anchor points for yourself, times when you remember to stop and just be in the present moment. Experience fully what you are doing or feeling, for example, when you drink a cup of something warm, eat, drive, or walk from your car to work.

Make a point of spending time with children and let them direct the play and the pace of exploration. Children can teach us about being in the moment.

SHARING THE STORY WITH OTHERS

Share with others what you feel, or see, or realize in your present-moment experiences.

forty-one

THE TRIAL OF GOD

Elie Wiesel (adapted)

Once, in a concentration camp during World War II, the Jewish people imprisoned there decided to put God on trial for failing to live up to his promises to protect them. Officiating at the trial were three rabbis, who appointed a lawyer for the people and a lawyer for God. There was much evidence introduced and many days of deliberation. Finally the verdict was read, and God was found guilty.

When the trial was over, the people were quiet. They looked at the rabbis and one person asked, "What do we do now?"

The only answer that made sense to the people, the only answer in the face of reality, was that they must pray.

~~~   ~~~   ~~~

YOUR STORY

Explore the story through meditation, visualization, writing, and/or an expressive art form.

It is not possible to read this story without re-entering the much larger story of the Holocaust. A simple story like this opens a window to the realities of a time that for most of us seems distant and difficult to fathom. Stepping into someone else's experience of suffering through story can help us to be more compassionate and open-minded. Reflecting on the spiritual trials of others informs our own experiences. Try to sit with the images of this story before moving to your own.

MAKING A PERSONAL CONNECTION WITH THE STORY

What personal meaning does this story have for you? While most of us today have not experienced terrors or loss such as those of the

Holocaust, we have faced times in our life when our faith was badly shaken. Who has not railed against God or asked, "Why?" The ending of this story calls us to question the nature of our relationship to our Creator. It makes us examine the nature of faith—faith as the way to God, faith as necessary to our psychic survival.

Looking back over your life, tell the story of your developing faith. If you have a personal relationship to God, how did this develop? When has that faith been questioned or broken? How has it mended? Describe times when you have put God on trial. What role has God played in your life and how has that changed over time?

TRYING ON THE IDEAS IN THE STORY

As you go through your week, notice the ways in which you relate to your Creator. Write a letter to God talking about your expectations of God's role in your life and in your soul's evolution. If you have a relationship to God, imagine your life without it.

SHARING THE STORY WITH OTHERS

People are always moved by this story. It takes them to some place bigger than words can express. See the index for other stories dealing with faith issues.

forty-two

THE KING AND HIS FALCON

Asia and Europe

One day long ago a king went hunting. On his forearm perched his favorite trained hunting falcon. His bird would fly high in the air, spot a rabbit or some other prey, and swoop down upon it, stunning or killing it for his master.

It had been a long day, and the king had left his hunting party and continued on alone far from home. By the end of the day the king was very thirsty and began to look for a place to drink.

At last he saw some water trickling over the edge of a high rock. He got down from his horse and unpacked his cup. As the king held his cup under the trickling drops, his pet falcon left his arm and flew overhead looking for prey. When the cup was nearly full, the king put it to his lips and was about to drink. All of a sudden his falcon swooped down and knocked the cup from his hands, spilling the water.

Annoyed, the king waved the bird away and began to fill his cup again. When it was half full he could wait no longer, and again put it to his lips. Again the bird swooped down and knocked the cup before he could drink.

"You imbecile!" he swore, as the bird alighted on a rock.

A third time the king filled his cup and a third time the bird knocked it away.

His anger growing into rage, the king declared that if the bird dared to knock the cup a fourth time, he would pay dearly. So saying, he got out his sword.

He filled his cup but a third of the way, and then put it to his lips. Again the falcon swooped down, but this time the king was ready. He sliced the bird as he passed, but not before the bird knocked the cup from his hand. The cup rolled past the dying bird and into an unreachable crevice.

Determined to quench his thirst, the king climbed up the steep rocky bank until, out of breath, he at last reached the spring. There it was, a pool of water; a pool of water in which a dead and very poisonous snake floated.

Then the king looked down at his dead bird, the bird that had saved his life. He climbed down and sadly put his loyal friend into his hunting bag. He rode slowly home that day, vowing never again to act in anger.

Your Story
Explore the story through meditation, visualization, writing, and/or an expressive art form.

Making a Personal Connection with the Story
Concentrating on his thirst, the king ignored his loyal pet's attempts to warn him and grew so angry that he killed the bird. Describe situations in which you have acted in anger because you were thwarted in getting something you craved. Can you think of situations in which you were able to stop long enough to perceive what was really going on?

The Buddhist monk and peace activist Thích Nhât Hanh suggests that we refrain from acting on our anger and focus on our breathing instead. He says that if we stay calm and look from a centered perspective on the situation that upsets us, we will see it eventually in the larger context. We may even see that the root of our anger is anger toward ourselves for being victims or failing in some way. Can you remember a situation when this may have been true for you?

Trying on the Ideas in the Story
As you go through your week, notice situations that anger you. Try the old idea of counting to ten, taking three deep breaths, or waiting an hour before responding. Step back to see what is at the root of your anger and your desire or craving.

Sharing the Story with Others
This is a good story for families to share in open discussions of how to express our anger in nondestructive ways.

forty-three

A DROP OF HONEY

Burma   and   Thailand

Once a king stood on his balcony eating honey on rice cakes with his chief adviser. As they ate, they gazed down on the street below. The king was in good humor that day, and as he laughed, a drop of honey fell from his rice cake onto the railing.

"Sire, you have spilled a drop of honey. Do let me wipe it up for you," offered his adviser.

"Oh, pay it no mind, my dear," said the king. "It's not our concern. The servants will clean it up later. I do not wish to be disturbed just now."

They went on eating and talking as the drop of honey warmed in the sun and began to slowly drip down the rail. At last it fell onto the street below.

Attracted by the sweet smell, a fly landed on it and began to eat.

"Your Highness," the adviser commented, "the drop of honey has now landed in the street and is attracting flies. Perhaps we should call someone to clean it."

"Pay it no mind," answered the king merrily. "It is not our concern."

Suddenly a gecko sprang out from under the palace, and ate the fly in one gulp.

Next a cat spied the gecko and pounced.

The cat playing with its food in the middle of the street caught the attention of a dog, who attacked it.

"Now, sire, there is a cat and dog fight in the street. Surely we should we call someone to stop it?" implored the adviser.

"Oh, pay it no mind," said the king. "Here come the cat and dog owners, they'll stop it. We don't need to get involved."

So the two continued to eat their honey and rice cakes and to watch the spectacle from their comfortable perch.

But below in the street, the cat's owner began beating the dog. The dog's owner then started to beat the cat. Soon the two were beating each other.

The king's good humor turned to anger as he watched the scene below. "I'll have no fighting in my streets," he bellowed. "Call in my guards to quell this battle at once!"

The palace guards were summoned. But by this time the fight had grown as friends on either side joined the fray. The guards tried to break up the fighting, but soon they too had joined in. With guards involved, the fight erupted into civil war. Houses were burned, and the palace itself was set afire and destroyed.

The kingdom was never returned to its former splendor, but new wisdom was gained in that country. Some people still say: We are each responsible for our actions, large and small. Small problems if unattended, grow into larger ones, and a whole kingdom can be lost from a drop of honey.

~ ~ ~

Your Story
Explore the story through meditation, visualization, writing, and/or an expressive art form.

Making a Personal Connection with the Story
Have you ever thought that some issue was not your problem only to discover that you were affected by it? Have you ever ignored little problems in a relationship until they felt too large to resolve? Share these stories with others.

This story has obvious social and political meaning. We have all heard the statement "If you are not part of the solution, you are part of the problem." How do you feel about that? What social or political issues do you feel powerless to change? Is there anything more you could do? What stops you?

Living in our modern society with its deluge of information can be overwhelming. We are disconnected from where our food, fuel, clothing, and other essentials come from and from where the refuse goes. We are inundated by the media's reports of the problems and tragedies of people all over the world. How do you take responsibility for your life as part of an entire cycle? How do you deal with the pain of the world? What do you do with the guilt occasioned by this pain? How does your lifestyle impact your spiritual life?

TRYING ON THE IDEAS IN THE STORY

The Buddha suggests that we should not only cause no harm but should take an interest in all the life around us, not just other people but plants, insects, etc. This week, pick a day to practice awareness of the actions of each moment and their consequences. Look at your actions and follow them to their conclusions. Notice all of the little and not so little opportunities to make something your problem, and try to act on some of these.

SHARING THE STORY WITH OTHERS

Make modern versions of this story with children or co-workers. For instance: "Once upon a time two kids were playing in the playground when one of them spit out a wad of gum," or "Once some government officials passed a law that only green-skinned persons could ride buses. The blue- and pink-skinned people protested, but the green skins said, 'It's not our problem.' "

forty-four

THE LOST KEY

Middle East

One night a neighbor strolling by Nasrudin's house found him outside under the street lamp brushing through the dust. "Have you lost something, my friend?" he asked. Nasrudin explained that he had lost his key and asked the neighbor to help him find it.

After some minutes of searching and turning up nothing, the neighbor asked him, "Are you sure you lost the key here?"

"No, I did not lose it here. I lost it inside the house," Nasrudin answered.

"If you lost the key in the house, Nasrudin, why are you looking for it out here?"

"Well, there's more light out here, of course," Nasrudin replied.

~~~ ~~~ ~~~

YOUR STORY

Explore the story through meditation, visualization, writing, and/or an expressive art form.

MAKING A PERSONAL CONNECTION WITH THE STORY

Keys open doors, start cars to carry you where you want to go, unlock treasure chests, private drawers, and journals. They also control who can go through doors.

Imagine, if you wish, that the key in the story represents a connection that you have lost. It may help to first imagine yourself as the innocent child that you were. For most of us, losing the connection has to do with being wounded as children. It can be difficult to remember details of when this wounding happened. Brainstorming on paper and sharing memories with siblings or friends are good ways to bring these memories to the forefront. Writing a letter to your child-self can be another good way to regain the key. Add to the story the ways in which you have rediscovered your keys along the way.

We are all looking for that which will give us access to greater freedom, equanimity, and peace. It was easier for Nasrudin to look where it was well lit for his key even though he knew it wasn't really there. Well-lit places may be the safe activities of life that keep us from our true paths. Where do you look for your lost key? Where do or did your parents and grandparents look for theirs? Where else can you look?

TRYING ON THE IDEAS IN THE STORY

As you go about your week, notice times in which you feel a sense of loss. Notice also the ways in which you search for what feels missing in you. Try to remember that you have only temporarily misplaced something so precious. Look for it in silence, in nature, among those who love you most for who you are. Take time this week to feel the longing and to acknowledge that the key is accessible and is your birthright.

Play with the imagery of keys and places where keys work, and create a waking dream story of your own as discussed in the introduction.

SHARING THE STORY WITH OTHERS

Tell Nasrudin tales. Tell your waking dream story. Tell your own version of this story, inserting your own personal key and where you are looking for it.

forty-five

THE THREE QUESTIONS

Zen

T here was once a king who decided that if he knew who the most important people to be with were, and what the most important thing to do was, and when the best time to do each thing was, that he would certainly be the finest king ever to rule the land. Although he had asked his advisers, none had been able to give him a good answer to these questions.

At last he decided to ask the advice of a wise hermit. The king dressed in the clothes of a commoner and set out for the forest. When he neared the hermit's hut, he ordered his knights to stay back at a distance, and he rode the last section of trail alone.

The king found the hermit digging in his garden. The old man greeted him but continued digging. The king told the hermit that he had come to find answers to his three questions. The hermit listened but gave no answer and continued working. The king observed that the hermit was frail and elderly and that the work was very difficult for him. The king offered to take over the digging, and the hermit allowed it.

The king dug for one hour. Then he repeated the question, but the hermit did not answer. He worked again for another hour, and then repeated his questions with the same results. This continued for a few more hours until the sun began to sink low in the sky. Finally the king got discouraged. "I came to you for answers wise man. If you have none, tell me and I will return home."

Just them someone came running up the path. They turned to see a man with his hands pressed to his stomach and blood flowing from between them. He dropped to the ground at the king's feet.

The king and the hermit knelt down and began tending to the man. The king washed and bandaged the man's wounds. The blood continued to flow so he kept having to change the bandages. The king also helped the hermit to get fresh water, and to help the man to drink.

Finally the man slept and did not wake until the next morning. The king too slept upon the ground, waking often to watch over the man. In the morning the man woke up and looked at the king.

"Forgive me," he said to the king.

"You have nothing to forgive me for," the king answered.

"Oh, but I do," he said. "You were my enemy, and I had sworn to take revenge on you for killing my brother and taking my land. I knew that you were coming here today and I decided to kill you on the trail. But when you did not return for many hours I left my hideout to find you. Your guards recognized me and wounded me. I escaped them but I would have bled to death if you had not cared for me. I meant to kill you but now you have saved my life. If I live I shall gladly serve you for the rest of my days."

The king was so happy to have been reconciled with an old enemy that he immediately forgave him and promised to return his land. Then the king called for his knights to carry the man back to his castle to be cared for by his own doctor.

After the wounded man had gone, the king asked the hermit once more if he would not give him the answer to his question.

"Your questions have already been answered." the hermit replied.

"But how?" the king answered, perplexed.

"How?" repeated the hermit. "If you had not taken pity on my weakness yesterday and helped me instead of returning home, that man would have ambushed and killed you on the trail. Therefore, the most important time was when you were digging my garden beds; and I was the most important person; and the most important thing to do was to do good for me. Later, when the man came running to us, the most important thing to do was to care for him. If you had not bound up his wounds he would have died without making peace with you. Therefore the most important person was that man, and what you did was the most important thing, and the right time was the time when you were doing it.

"You see, the most important time is always the present moment. It is the only time that is important because it is the only time that we have control over. The past we can only look back on and wish that we had done differently. The future we can only imagine. The most important person is always the one you are with in the present moment, and the only important deed is the deed that does what is best for others."

At last the king understood. He returned to rule wisely one moment at a time.

Your Story
Explore the story through meditation, visualization, writing, and/or an expressive art form.

Making a Personal Connection with the Story
We all have stories about times when we wished to be somewhere else, doing something else, with someone else, but which turned out to be very important for us. Make a list of situations in which you feel impatient. Imagine ways of being in those situations in which you honor them as the most important.

Trying on the Ideas in the Story
This week try to be aware of being right where you are supposed to be in the present moment, not impatient to be doing things that feel more productive. Instead of doing laundry to get it done, do laundry to enjoy the doing.

The only time that you have control over is the present moment. If you live well in that moment, all present moments can be well lived. Practice having well-lived present moments this week.

SHARING THE STORY WITH OTHERS

You may wish to introduce or end the story on a humorous note with several examples of moments when you have little patience, such as sitting in traffic, spending time with a relative you dislike. Then, if possible, share an example of how one of those tedious moments became transforming. Others may want to share their tedious and transforming moments as well.

f o r t y - s i x

THE WOUNDED HEALER

The Talmud

There once was a rabbi who wanted to know when the Messiah would come and how he would know him. One day he came upon Elijah and asked him these questions.

Elijah answered, "You must go and ask him yourself."

"Is he here on earth?"

"Yes."

"But where will I find him?" asked the rabbi.

Elijah answered that he must go to the gates of the city and look among the poorest people there who are covered with wounds.

"But there are so many poor and wounded," worried the rabbi. "How will I know him?"

"You will know him," Elijah answered. "For the others unbind all of their wounds at the same time and then bind them up again. The Messiah, however, unbinds one wound at a time and binds it up again, all the while saying to himself, 'Perhaps someone will need me; I must be ready.' "

YOUR STORY

Explore the story through meditation, visualization, writing, and/or an expressive art form.

MAKING A PERSONAL CONNECTION WITH THE STORY

We are all wounded. And we are all needed to help heal the wounds of others and the wounds of the world. What are your beliefs concerning how "healed" you must be before you are qualified to heal or help others?

Tell the stories of how your wounds have led you to be a helper for others.

How do you "bind up" your wounds so that you can attend to the needs of others without imposing your own pain and confusion? How do you "unbind" them to work on self-healing?

TRYING ON THE IDEAS IN THE STORY

As you go through your week, be aware of this process of binding up and unbinding your own wounds. Plan to make space for both this week.

SHARING THE STORY WITH OTHERS

This is a particularly appropriate story for people in the helping professions, but all of us need to be reminded that we can be of service even though we are still healing.

forty-seven

FEATHERS

Jewish

L ong ago, in a small village in eastern Europe, there lived a man who had a terrible habit of gossiping. His talk had hurt various people in the town. One of these people came to the rabbi seeking justice. The rabbi called the two together.

"You've ruined my reputation," the victim charged.

"I'm sorry," said the man. "I'll take back my words and then all will be well."

"You can't take back your words," the victim cried.

"Of course I can," the man responded.

The rabbi saw that the gossip did not understand the extent of the damage done, and so he decided to use action, which often speaks louder than words.

"If you wish to right this wrong and be forgiven for your gossiping," he said, "you must come to the village square tomorrow with your feather pillow."

The man was perplexed, but secretly hopeful that he had gotten off easily with the loss of only a pillow.

The next day he arrived at the village square.

"Here," said the rabbi, handing him a pair of shears. "Cut the pillow and let the feathers fly out, each and every one."

Still bewildered, the man did as he was instructed until every feather flew about the square. Some came quickly down, while others lifting on air currents traveled above the walls of the square.

"Now," commanded the rabbi, "bring me back the feathers, every single one."

The man looked upon him as if he were crazy. "I cannot catch all of these feathers. Some are near, but some have already gone over the wall. They've gone into every nook and cranny, it would be impossible to gather them all."

"Impossible," agreed the rabbi, "like trying to take back the words from the rumor you spread. Who knows how far it has traveled and where it will go next?"

Understanding the effect of his actions at last, the man returned to the victim's house and apologized. He never spoke harmful words of another again.

~~~   ~~~   ~~~

Your Story
Explore the story through meditation, visualization, writing, and/or an expressive art form.

Making a Personal Connection with the Story
It has been said, "When we truly understand the effects of our actions we will cease to act harmfully."

Remember times when you have talked negatively about another and how they have been hurt by it. Remember times when others have spread negative rumors about you and how you felt. Share these stories with others.

Trying the Ideas in the Story
Be aware of your conversations as you go through this week. How often do you talk negatively about others? Notice whether this kind of gossiping is done to build a sense of connection with the ones you are talking to, or out of jealousy, anger, or some other reason.

Notice also why you choose to speak positively about some people. Whether you judge someone positively or negatively, you are making the statement that you too are fair game for judgment and comparison.

Take a fast this week from speaking negatively of others. Hold your tongue instead and try to see them through compassionate eyes.

Sharing the Story with Others
You can tell people when necessary that you are endeavoring not to speak ill of others and can tell them the story to explain why.

forty-eight

THE BAG OF GOLD

Hindu

Siva and Shakti, the Divine Couple in Hinduism, are in their heavenly abode watching over the earth. They are touched by the challenges of human life, the complexity of human reactions, and the ever-present place of suffering in the human experience. As they watch, Shakti spies a miserably poor old man walking down the road. His clothes are shabby and his sandals are tied together with rope. Her heart is wrung with compassion. Touched by his goodness and his struggle, Shakti turns to her divine husband and begs him to give this man some gold. Siva looks at the man for a long moment. "My dearest Wife," he says, "I cannot do that." Shakti is astounded. "Why, what do you mean, Husband? You are Lord of the Universe. Why can't you do this simple thing?"

"I cannot give this to him because he is not yet ready to receive it," Siva replies. Shakti becomes angry. "Do you mean to say that you cannot drop a bag of gold in his path?"

"Surely I can," Siva replies, "but that is quite another thing."

"Please, Husband," says Shakti.

And so Siva drops a bag of gold in the man's path.

The man meanwhile walks along thinking to himself, "I wonder if I will find dinner tonight—or shall I go hungry again?" Turning a bend in the road, he sees something on the path in his way. "Aha," he says. "Look there, a large rock. How fortunate that I have seen it. I might have torn these poor sandals of mine even further." And carefully stepping over the bag of gold, he goes on his way.

Your Story

Explore the story through meditation, visualization, writing, and/or an expressive art form.

Making a Personal Connection with the Story

Bags of gold are constantly rolling, careening, or crashing into our paths, but we do not always name them as such. Only through the process of looking back in wonder and taking the time to recollect the events of our lives as part of one larger story are we able to know the gold that we have been given and to see that within each stumbling block there is something of value.

Looking at your life today, what conditions exist that look and feel like rocks, boulders, or avalanches blocking or slowing your way? Try to imagine what learning could come from them to reveal their gold. Brainstorm about previous times in your life when you—like the old man in the story—carefully avoided rocks on the road of life to keep yourself safe. Did you ever stay in a bad relationship too long or not dare to commit to a good one? Do you have unfulfilled dreams of developing your talents or taking a big risk in your career?

We all have *profound* experiences of grace—bags of gold—at many times during our lives, but we do not often honor them as such. Brainstorm about times when you have experienced grace. Perhaps you experienced an unexpected love for or from someone or found great peace in natural surroundings. Perhaps you have experienced a powerful learning or healing. Grace is defined here as an experience of feeling God's presence or love or help very deeply. Shape these experiences into stories with clear imagery and feeling so that you can recall them clearly and can return to the experience of grace again and again.

Trying on the Ideas in the Story

This week try to see the gold hidden in every experience no matter how small or trying. Before going to sleep each night, write about all of the gold encountered during the day. You will feel quite rich.

Try the following visualization while sitting or walking. Imagine that you are setting all of your gold upon a huge table. One at a time, think about the various aspects of your life—relationships, births, learning, trans-

formations, gifts and talents, material wealth, experiences in natural surroundings or with spirit. Set your blessings upon the table and feel how rich
you are. You may wish to transform this visualization into something physically artistic, such as a sculpture or dance.

SHARING THE STORY WITH OTHERS

Have a "Grace Happens" gathering where you share your "bags of gold."
People greatly appreciate opportunities to hear one another's stories of
learning and transformation. It helps them to be aware of, to remember,
and to honor their own.

forty-nine

THE LEGEND OF THE MISTLETOE

Scandinavia

Of all the Nordic gods and goddesses, Baldur was the most beloved. This beautiful, radiant bringer of mercy and kindness was the wisest arbiter of every dispute. The delicate chamomile flower became his emblem, for his gentleness was felt by all.

Beloved as he was, Baldur was not free from despair. Night after night he was visited by terrible dreams of gloom and grief. At last he went to his mother, Frigga, in hopes that she might lift the sorrow from his heart. When Frigga looked into her son's eyes she became filled with dread, for she saw that he was being courted by the cold shadow of death. So began a mother's journey to protect her son. Frigga traveled throughout each of the nine worlds gathering oaths from all things: fire, water, iron, and stone. Each plant and every disease, all things swore to Frigga that they would do nothing to harm her son. When she returned home, these oaths were put to a test.

Hermod, bold messenger of the gods, was the first to challenge the power of the oath. He threw his mighty battle-ax at Baldur. It hurtled through the air, but the metal of the blade and the wood of the handle withheld their power. The ax dropped harmlessly at his feet. Then a mighty shout of joy rose from the gods. Baldur, whom they loved, was safe! They spent the day on the plain known as the Peacestead, hurling knives and stones at their invincible target. In the midst of it all stood Baldur, radiant and shining as around him fell useless every kind of weapon god or man could devise.

But there are some who don't like beauty; some whose feelings twist at unvarnished joy. Among the Nordic gods, that one is called Loki and he looked for a way to end the happiness. He sidled over to Baldur's blind brother Hod and soon discovered that Frigga's work had caused this unnatural state of affairs.

Loki transformed himself into an old woman and hobbled off to Frigga's halls to talk with her. "May I come in?" Loki quavered. "I've traveled a long way and I've just seen a terrible sight." Frigga welcomed the old woman in and called for refreshments. They sat down together and Loki spoke. "There is a terrible sport going on at Peacestead. All the gods are ganging up on one man, throwing their spears and weapons at him."

Frigga smiled at the old woman and said kindly, "The one they are throwing weapons at is my son Baldur, and he cannot be harmed. I have taken an oath from all things never to hurt him."

"How like a mother's love to leave nothing to chance," said Loki. "Still, for your sake, I hope you asked absolutely *everything* to swear."

Frigga's eyes grew soft. "I've gathered oaths from all except the mistletoe that grows west of Valhalla. It seemed too young to give an oath."

"Yes, I'm sure it's much too young," Loki simpered. "But look, how the light is fading! I really must be on my way." The old woman hobbled outside and transformed into Loki. As darkness descended he raced west to find the mistletoe.

In those times, the mistletoe grew from the ground. Loki uprooted it, stripped it of its leaves, and sharpened one end to a point. Then he hurried off to the Peacestead. When he arrived there, he grimaced with delight. Frigga herself had come to watch the gaming. Loki sauntered over to Hod, who was standing disconsolate in a corner.

"Hod, doesn't it feel terrible to be left out of all the fun? Doesn't it make you angry that everyone has forgotten you? But here, I've got a little dart for you. Close your fingers around it and I'll guide your hand. Throw it at your brother!"

The mistletoe dart flew through the air and pierced Baldur's chest. It went deep into his heart, and the god of light collapsed lifeless. The terrible dream had come true.

Frigga, weeping, cradled her son's body. As her tears fell, they became gentle white berries on the barren twig. Despair lay in everyone's heart, for the best and the beautiful had been taken. Still, Frigga would not give in. She sent Hermod to Hela's kingdom of death to plead for Baldur's return. There, in death's kingdom Hermod spoke silver-tongued words to the grim goddess herself. "Hela, I have come to plead for one who is greatly missed; and I mean Baldur, who belongs among us, and whom we cannot live without."

"I am not sure Baldur is as beloved as you would have me believe," Hela rasped. "We shall put it to the test. Since hatred and malice brought about his end, then let everyone give up their long-standing grievances and their evil thoughts in exchange for his return. If all will let go of memories of past wrongs and clear a place of forgiveness in their hearts, then Hela shall not hold Baldur back."

When fleet Hermod returned with the message for the gods, Frigga stood filled with the blessing of relief. "I will be the first to open my heart for my son's return," she said. "And as a token of this, the mistletoe which has slain my son I raise up to a special place of honor. No longer shall it grow out of the earth, but it shall be supported by the great oak, suspended between heaven and earth. And whoever meets beneath it, be they enemy or friend, shall embrace and forgive and open their hearts one to the other."

～ ～ ～

Your Story

Explore the story through meditation, visualization, writing, and/or an expressive art form.

Making a Personal Connection with the Story

Forgiving others begins with cultivating new ways of seeing ourselves. According to Ernest Kurtz and Katherine Ketchem, authors of *The Spirituality of Imperfection*, forgiveness involves "letting go of the past—giv-

ing up the claim to control the past and refusing to be controlled by it."
This involves forgiving yourself for having been or felt like a victim, and
letting go of any anger you hold toward yourself for having been vulnerable or culpable.

Forgiveness does not necessarily mean loving or embracing another, and
it certainly doesn't mean forgetting the past. But once we have learned to
be compassionate toward ourselves and our imperfections, and once we can
see our life's experiences as part of the big picture, we can extend compassion to all human beings. It is a circular process in which forgiveness of others allows us to be more accepting of ourselves.

If you had to forgive everyone against whom you hold grudges to bring
back to life what is most dear to you, who would be on your list?

If you had to forgive yourself for past actions, perceived failures, vul-
nerabilities, and inadequacies, what would be on your list?

Trying on the Ideas in the Story

Look at your list of people and situations that require forgiveness this week
and see where you could clear past wounds. Notice the opportunities, large
and small, to forgive or hold no malice in daily life. Notice how it feels not
to allow yourself to be a victim or to be controlled by the past. Visualize
yourself literally clearing a place in your heart for greater levels of compassion, equanimity, and love to enter.

Sharing the Story with Others

This is a perfect story for the winter solstice/Christmas season. And it's a
great story to share with groups of people who are in community with one
another.

f i f t y

JESUS' CLOAK

Christian

Now there was a woman who had been suffering from hemorrhages for twelve years. She had endured much under many physicians, and had spent all that she had; and she was no better, but rather grew worse.

She had heard about Jesus, and so she came up behind him in the crowd and touched his cloak, for she said, "If I but touch his clothes, I will be made well." Immediately her hemorrhaging stopped; and she felt in her body that she was healed of her disease.

Immediately aware that power had gone forth from him, Jesus turned about in the crowd and said, "Who touched my clothes?" And his disciples said to him, "You see the crowd pressing in on you; how can you say, 'Who touched me?'"

He looked all around to see who had done it. But the woman, knowing what had happened to her, came in fear and trembling, fell down before him, and told him the whole truth. He said to her, "Daughter, your faith has made you well; go in peace, and be healed of your disease."

～ ～ ～

YOUR STORY
Explore the story through meditation, visualization, writing, and/or an expressive art form.

MAKING A PERSONAL CONNECTION WITH THE STORY
If you do not feel comfortable relating to Christian stories, I suggest that you read miracle stories of the spiritual traditions that you can

relate to. Legends of the Baal Shem Tov, Habib the Muslim, and the Buddha, and stories from many American Indian cultures, for example, are rich with miracles.

What are your favorite miracle stories, whether from real life, religion, or fiction? How do you define what constitutes a miracle? If you are unclear here, think about transcendent experiences, both within yourself and in the outside world, in which there is an experience of the sacred, a sudden transformation, a new spark of understanding. You may also wish to focus on the miracle of life itself, the workings of our bodies and all the things we take for granted. Describe your personal experiences of miracles.

Miracle stories may evoke different reactions in us. We love to hear of seemingly miraculous healings and occurrences because they lift our spirits as we imagine new possibilities and feel new hope. This said, after all the miraculous healing stories we read or hear about and all the miracles that surround us daily, we are mostly forgetful of the power that makes these things happen. We may actually be skeptical about miracles, trusting only in the changes within ourselves and others that come with hard work and time. Why do you think this is?

This story offers a way to think about our role in making miracles happen. Jesus told the woman that it was her faith that had made her well. The woman's faith caused her to go and get what she needed, and to believe that it was possible. Sometimes passively waiting for a miracle can keep us from doing what is needed to make things happen through faith. In his book *Conversations with God,* Neale Donald Walsch says that God asks us to look at the "sponsoring thoughts" that are behind all that we believe in. We may say that we want to be successful, or healthy, or prosperous, or compassionate, but we may hold limiting beliefs underneath about what is possible for us or between us and our Creator. What does absolute faith mean to you? What do you believe in with no uncertainty? Do you believe, for instance, that you will be taken care of no matter what? That you are a treasured and sacred being?

How has your faith changed over time? Write or tell the autobiography of your faith. What experiences have strengthened or weakened it? What things do you now have faith in that you did not trust before? How did this come about?

TRYING ON THE IDEAS IN THE STORY

As you go through the week, be aware of the miracles of life that you may usually take for granted. Focus on a different aspect of nature a day—for instance, the miracles of our brains, of birth, or the cycles of nature. Practice being filled full of wonder and faith by the awareness of these miracles. Ask other people what miracles they have experienced or heard of. Make a "miracles" collage on a wall of your home.

Take a look at your faith in God and God's creative, healing power this week. Spend some time writing down the things that you would like to transform in your inner and outer worlds and listen to your inner voice for your "sponsoring thoughts."

As you go through your week, imagine that Jesus, Mother Teresa, the Buddha, the Baal Shem, or your particular beloved or hero is walking beside you at all times. Seek their counsel in all matters. Hold on to the hem of their gown and ask for healing.

SHARING THE STORY WITH OTHERS

Tell the miracle stories that you relate to. Help others to share their stories and to honor the miracles of daily life.

fifty-one

"YOU'RE STILL CARRYING HER"

Z e n

Once two Buddhist monks were on a journey to a distant monastery when they came to a river. There on the bank sat a young woman. "I beg you," she asked, "could you carry me across? The current is strong today and I'm afraid I might be swept away."

The first monk remembered his vows never to look at or touch a woman, and so, without so much as a nod, he crossed through the heavily flowing currents and soon reached the other side.

The other monk showed compassion and bent down so that the woman could climb upon his back to cross the river. Although she was slight, the current was strong and the rocky bottom made it difficult crossing. Reaching the other side, he let the woman down and went on his way.

After some hours journeying down the dusty road in silence the first monk could no longer contain his anger at the second for breaking their vows. "How could you look at that woman?" he blurted out. "How could you touch her, let alone carry her across the river? You've put our reputation at stake."

The first monk looked at his companion and smiled. "I put that woman down way back there at the river bank, but I see that you're still carrying her."

~ ~ ~

YOUR STORY

Explore the story through meditation, visualization, writing, and/or an expressive art form.

Making a Personal Connection with the Story

What stands out for you in this story?

There is a saying, "Religion is for those who are afraid of going to hell, and spirituality is for those who have been there." What religious rules did you learn as a child? What governs your spiritual practice?

There may be times when we have to choose between rules and heart. There may be times when we have to make decisions that will be unpopular.

Can you remember times when you have made decisions and have let them go while others chastised you? Can you remember times when you chastised yourself and carried your burden way past the river?

Very few of us escape stress in these fast-paced times. Much of stress arises from the rules that have been governing us since we were born: We shouldn't do this, or we have to live up to that. Most of us carry feelings of guilt and disappointment and judgments of others way past the place and time when they occurred. Describe times in which this has been true for you.

Trying on the Ideas in the Story

As you go through the week, if you notice yourself feeling guilty, or angry at yourself, notice what rules are governing your thoughts and calling you up short. Sometimes we can hear the rules through our "parent" voices. Make a conscious effort to leave experiences of guilt or shortcoming where they happened. Try to let a more compassionate parent voice emerge. When you feel tense, remember the monk who left the woman at the river bank and did not trouble himself about her afterwards, and try to do the same.

Sharing the Story with Others

Sharing this story with others can generate an exchange of experiences in which we acted from our hearts rather than by the rules. It can also be the start of a great discussion about what our internal rules are, where they came from, and how to change them. It can serve as a great stress reducer. "Leave your burdens at the river!"

fifty-two

THE QUESTION

Hasidic

T here is a story about the great Hasidic master Rabbi Zusya. When Rabbi Zusya grew old and knew that his time on earth was nearing a close, his students were called around him. Timidly one of them spoke and asked Rabbi Zusya what he was most afraid of about dying.

"I am most afraid of what they will ask me when I get to heaven," he answered.

"What will they ask you?" the disciples were eager to know.

"They will not ask me, 'Zusya, why were you not like Moses?' " he answered. "They will ask me, 'Zusya, why were you not Zusya?' "

~ ~ ~

YOUR STORY
Explore the story through meditation, visualization, writing, and/or an expressive art form.

MAKING A PERSONAL CONNECTION WITH THE STORY
If you were Zusya, how would you answer the question put to him in heaven?

This story brings us full circle back to the questions posed in the introduction about our personal vision, and to the questions posed in the first story about living our dharma. Look back to what you wrote then and compare it to how you are feeling now.

Imagine the story of what it would be like to be totally you. This is not as simple for many of us as it sounds. We may be out of touch with our inner voices or we may have been living so long within the constraints of socially acceptable behavior that we can't quite imagine what would make us who we really are. Perhaps this achievement of becoming totally oneself needs to be tackled in gradual steps. Begin with increased self-awareness and then self-acceptance.

It has been said that we can only be as loving toward the world as we are toward ourselves. Describe the parts of yourself that you do love and honor. Describe the parts for which you still feel shame and denial. How can you accept these parts of yourself more fully?

TRYING ON THE IDEAS IN THE STORY

As you go about your week, notice when you are expressing what feels true for you and when you are not. Notice how you feel and try to accept it without judgment. Imagine what you would do and how your life would be if you were "totally you." This does not mean the "ideal" you at 115 pounds or making sixty grand a year. It is a picture of what you would be like if the inner you were totally satisfied and expressed. Turn this into a movie that you can picture in your mind in great detail. View it over and over until you can feel it to be possible.

SHARING THE STORY WITH OTHERS

Let others tell you their true-self stories.

NOTES

~

INTRODUCTION

1. The hide-and-seek story with God is a folktale whose origins I am unable to find. A longer written version in which "truth" is hidden appears in *What We May Be: Techniques for Psychological and Spiritual Growth Through Psychosynthesis,* by Piero Ferruci (Los Angeles: J. P. Tarcher, 1982), 143. Ferruci attributes it to Eastern origins.

2. "Hide and Seek," retold by Elisa Davy Pearmain from *Tales of the Hasidim: The Early Masters/The Later Masters,* by Martin Buber, translated by Olga Marx, copyright 1947, 1948, copyright renewed by Schocken Books, Inc., p. 97. Reprinted by permission of Schocken Books, distributed by Pantheon Books, a division of Random House, Inc..

3. The Korean Zen master story comes from the book *Seeking the Heart of Wisdom,* by Joseph Goldstein and Jack Kornfield (Boston: Shambhala Publications, 1987), 75–76. Retold with the generous permission of Shambhala.

4. "The Shortest Distance," reprinted from "Myths," in *One Minute Wisdom,* by Anthony de Mello, S.J., Copyright 1985, p. 23. Used by permission of Doubleday, a division of Bantam Doubleday Dell Publishing Group, Inc.

5. *The Song of the Bird,* by Anthony de Mello (New York: Doubleday, 1982), 1.

6. U.S. Department of Education: "What Works: Research about Teaching and Learning" (Washington, D.C.: Department of Education, 1986), 23.

7. Elizabeth Hill, "Words Are Truly Holy." An interview with Clarissa Pinkola Estés in *Storytelling* magazine (Jonesborough, Tenn.: National Storytelling Association, July 1977), 10.

8. "Meat of the Tongue," retold by Elisa Davy Pearmain. Written sources for this story can be found in *Legends of the Swahili,* by Jan Knappert (London: Heinemann, 1970), and *Apples from Heaven,* by Naomi Baltuck (New Haven, Conn: Linnet Books, 1995), 113–15.

9. *Frames of Mind: The Theory of Multiple Intelligences,* by Howard Gardner (New York: Basic Books, 1983), 73–276.

STORY WATER

The poem "Story Water," by Jelaluddin Rumi of Turkey, the thirteenth-century mystical Sufi poet, is from *The Essential Rumi,* by Coleman Barks (San Francisco: Harper SanFrancisco, 1995), 171–72. Reprinted with the kind permission of the author.

THE STORIES

1. "The Monk and the Scorpion," retold by Elisa Davy Pearmain. I first heard this story on an inspirational audiotape series by Wayne Dyer, who gave me permission to use it. I have not found a written source.

2. "The Good Samaritan," retold by Elisa Davy Pearmain from the New Testament, Luke 10:25–37, New Revised Standard Version, © 1989 by the Division of Christian Education of the National Council of the Churches of Christ in the U.S.A. New Revised Standard Version, © 1989 by the Division of Christian Education of the National Council of the Churches of Christ in the U.S.A.

3. "That Is Good," adapted by Elisa Davy Pearmain with the permission of the publisher from C. Witherell and N. Noddings, eds., *Stories Lives Tell: Narrative and Dialogue in Education* (New York: Teachers College Press, Columbia University, 1991), 118–20. All rights reserved. This is a story from India told to Kirin Narayan. This folktale motif has many variants coming from countries as diverse as China and Africa.

4. "Abou Ben Adhem," by Leigh Hunt, an English writer who lived from 1784 to 1859. This story can be found in many collections of narrative poetry or English poets of the nineteenth century. See several collections, including *Best Loved Story Poems,* by Walter E. Thwing (Garden City, N.Y.: Garden City Publishing Co., 1941), and *The Home Book of Verse,* by Burton Egbert Stevenson (New York: Holt, Rinehart & Winston, 1912), 2999. I also found a Sufi version of this story in *The Way of the Sufi,* by Idries Shah (London: Octagon Press 1980), 238, which may have been the source of inspiration for Hunt.

5. "Leave Your Name on the Door," retold by Elisa Davy Pearmain. Versions of this tale can be found in *The Exploits of the Incomparable Mulla Nasrudin,* by Idries Shah (New York: Simon & Schuster, 1966), 26, and *Stories of the Spirit, Stories of the Heart,* by Jack Kornfield and Christina Feldman (New York: HarperCollins, 1991), 262.

6. "Speak Only Praise," retold with permission from *Living Each Day,* by Rabbi Abraham J. Twerski, from The ArtScroll Series (Brooklyn, N.Y.: Mesorah Publications, 1988), 71.

7. "The Cricket Story," adapted with permission from Rhona Leventhal, a storyteller, creative movement and drama specialist, and educator who travels nationally and abroad telling stories and presenting workshops for teachers, adults and children. Rhona first published this story in *Spinning Tales, Weaving Hope,* edited by Ed Brody et al., *The Stories for World Change Network* (Philadelphia: New Society Publishers, 1992), 201. Rhona thinks it may be a contemporary American Indian tale.

8. "The Dervish in the Ditch," retold by Elisa Davy Pearmain with the permission of storyteller/author Doug Lipman, from whom she first heard the story. This story can be found on Doug's audiotape *Milk from the Bull's Horn: Tales of Nurturing Men* (Cambridge, Mass.: Yellow Moon Press, 1986). See the resources section at the back of the book for information on Doug and Yellow Moon Press. The quote in "Jesus' Purse" is from "The Answer of Jesus," by Attar of Nishapur, found in *The Way of the Sufi,* by Idries Shah (London: Octagon Press, 1980), 63.

9. "How the Spider Symbol Came to the People," retold with permission from *Keepers of the Animals,* by Joseph Bruchac and Michael Caduto (Golden, Colo.:

Fulcrum Publishing, 1990), 31. Contact Fulcrum at 350 Indiana St., Ste. 350, 80401, 1-800-992-2908.

10. "This, Too, Shall Pass," retold by Elisa Davy Pearmain. Variants on this tale may be found in the following collections: *Tales from the Wise Men of Israel*, by Judith ish-Kishor (New York: J. B. Lippincott Co., 1962), 19–26; *The Way of the Sufi*, by Idries Shah (London: Octagon Press, 1980); and *Folktales of Israel*, ed. Dov Noy (Chicago: University of Chicago Press, 1963), 174; and *The Classic Tales : 4,000 Years of Jewish Lore*, by Ellen Franjel (Northvale, N.J.: Jason Aronson, 1989), 257. Storyteller Heather Forest has a lovely version on her audiotape *The Eye of the Beholder* (Cambridge, Mass.: Yellow Moon Press, 1991).

11. "The Bundle of Sticks," retold by Elisa Davy Pearmain. Found in many collections of Aesop's fables, including *Aesop's Fables*, by Vernon Jones (New York: Avenel Books, 1912), 49; *Aesop and Company*, by Barbara Bader (New York: Houghton Mifflin, 1991); and *Aesop's Fables*, by Louis Untermeyer (New York: Golden Press, 1965).

12. "Catch the Wind," from *The Wisdom of the Desert*, by Thomas Merton, Copyright 1960 The Abbey of Gethsemani, Inc. Reprinted with permission of New Directions Publishing Corporation, New York. I do not have a written source for "Do Not Open the Door." I heard it told during a meditation workshop.

13. "What Is Heaven, What Is Hell," retold by Elisa Davy Pearmain. I first heard this story from storyteller John Porcino. Written variants may be found in "The Monk and the Samurai," by John Porcino, in *Spinning Tales, Weaving Hope*, edited by Ed Brody et al. (Philadelphia: New Society Publishers, 1992); "The Gates of Paradise," in *Zen Flesh, Zen Bones: A Collection of Zen and Pre-Zen Writings*, by Paul Reps (Rutland, Vt.: Charles Tuttle Co., 1957), 71; *Zen Buddhism* (Mount Vernon, N.Y.: Peter Pauper Press, 1959), 21; and *One Hand Clapping: Zen Stories for All Ages*, by Rafe Martin (New York: Rizzoli International Publications, 1995), 13.

14. "The Buried Treasure," retold by Elisa Davy Pearmain. This story is widely told and probably has Sufi origins. Idries Shah attributes the story to Hasan of Basra, who lived nearly twelve hundred years ago. Versions can be found in *Tales of the Dervishes*, by Idries Shah (New York: E. P. Dutton & Co., 1969), 144, and *Aesop's Fables*, by Vernon Jones (New York: Avenel Books, 1912), 45. Ruth Sawyer has an Italian variant in *The Way of the Storyteller* (New York: Penguin Books, 1942), 219. I also mentioned the book *Eight Weeks to Optimum Health*, by Andrew Weil, M.D. (New York: Alfred A. Knopf, 1997).

15. "The Peddler of Swaffham" is a legend with variants from English, Irish, and Hebrew sources. The English version is widely told in the storytelling community and published in the following sources: *British Folktales*, by Katherine Briggs (New York: Pantheon Books, 1977), 244–45, and *British Folktales*, by Kevin Crosley-Holland (New York: Orchard Books, 1987), 251–64. According to Crosley-Holland this is a true story. With his treasure, Chapman had the church in Swaffham rebuilt. His stone statue stands before it to this day. The story is recorded in the "Black Book," which is kept in the Swaffham church library.

Ruth Sawyer includes an Irish version of this story, "The Peddler of Ballaghadereen," in her book *The Way of the Storyteller* (New York: Penguin Books,

1942), 239. In the Irish version the peddler dreams of St. Patrick, who points the way in the dream. He too builds a church at the crossroads. Sawyer believes that this story came originally from Hebrew sources attributed to the lost books of the Apocrypha. She notes a written version of this story by M. R. James in his book *Old Testament Legends.* Other Jewish sources include *Jewish Stories One Generation Tells Another,* by Penina Schram (Northvale, N.J.: Jason Aronson, 1993); and *Challah and Latkes* (an audiotaped version), by Cindy Rivka Marshall (Newton Highlands, Mass.: Cindy Marshall Productions, 1997) (PO Box 610143, 02161). I first heard this story from storyteller Jay O'Callahan. You can find his version on his videotape *A Master Class with Jay O'Callahan,* Vineyard Video, 1-800-626-5356.

16. "God Sends a Lifeboat," retold by Elisa Davy Pearmain. This story is in the oral tradition. I have never seen a written version. I first heard it from storyteller and pastor Jennifer Justice, who overheard it being told one evening in a restaurant.

17. "The Rich Man's Treasures," adapted by Elisa Davy Pearmain from Matthew 25:14–30 and Luke 19:11–27, New Revised Standard Version, © 1989 by the Division of Christian Education of the National Council of the Churches of Christ in the U.S.A.

18. "The Empty Cup," retold by Elisa Davy Pearmain. I first heard this story told by Wayne Dyer. There are a number of written sources for it, including *Zen Flesh, Zen Bones,* by Paul Reps (Rutland, Vt.: Charles Tuttle Co., 1957), 19; *Zen Buddhism* (Mount Vernon, N.Y: Peter Pauper Press, 1959), 30; and *Wisdom Tales from around the World,* by Heather Forest (Little Rock: August House, 1996), 41.

19. "My Sins Are Running Out behind Me," from Thomas Merton, *The Wisdom of the Desert,* Copyright 1960 The Abbey of Gethsemani, Inc., p. 40. Reprinted with permission of New Directions Publishing Corporation, N.Y. "Casting the First Stone," adapted by Elisa Davy Pearmain from John 8:1–11, New Revised Standard Version, © 1989 by the Division of Christian Education of the National Council of the Churches of Christ in the U.S.A.

20. "The Lion's Whisker," retold by Elisa Davy Pearmain. Written variants in print include *The Lion's Whisker: Tales of High Africa,* by Brent Ashabranner and Russell Davis (Boston: Little, Brown & Co., 1950); *African Village Folktales,* by Edna Mason Kaulu (New York: World Publishing Co., 1968); and *The Lion's Whisker* (a picture book), retold by Nancy Raines Day (New York: Scholastic, 1995). These tales are usually attributed to the Amhara people of Ethiopia. A Korean variant can be found in *The Tiger's Whisker,* by Harold Courlander (New York: Harcourt, Brace & World, 1968). Clarissa Pinkola Estés tells a Japanese version called "The Tiger's Eyelash" in her audiotape *Women Who Run with Wolves,* published by Sounds True Productions, Boulder, Colo., 1-800-333-9185.

21. "The Most Beautiful Song," reprinted with the permission of Simon & Schuster, Inc., from *The Forest People,* by Colin Turnbull, Copyright (1961), renewed 1989 by Colin Turnbull, pp. 82–83. You can find this story also in *African Village Folktales,* by Edna Mason Kaula (New York: World Publishing Company, 1968), 110–17.

22. I heard "The Quail's Song" told long ago and have not been able to locate a written version. It may be a distant cousin to a Jataka tale in which a flock of quail learn

to outsmart a hunter by flying together to free themselves from the net, but then squabble among themselves and are trapped. See "A Flock of Birds," in *Wisdom Tales from around the World,* by Heather Forest (Little Rock: August House, 1996), 17.

23. "The Lost Ticket," retold by Elisa Davy Pearmain. I first heard the poet Coleman Barks tell this story. He prefaced it by saying that stories are still being created about Nasrudin today. Thanks to Coleman for permission to pass it on.

24. "A Mustard Seed," retold by Elisa Davy Pearmain. It is said that the wise man in this story was the Buddha and that the grieving mother later became one of his disciples. A Saudi Arabian version of this story called "The Bedouin and the Gazelle" can be found in *Arab Folktales,* ed. and trans. Inea Bushnaq (New York: Pantheon Books, 1986), 44–45. Jane Yolen also includes it in her collection *Favorite Folktales from around the World* (New York: Pantheon Books, 1986), 415–16. I first heard this story from storyteller Ron O'Reilly at a time when I really needed it.

25. "The Castle Door" is an original story by Elisa Davy Pearmain, inspired by the Rumi poem "The Beloved's Door." Significantly different translations of this poem can be found in *The Way of the Sufi,* by Idries Shah (London: Octagon Press, 1980), 189, and *We Are Three,* by Coleman Barks (Athens, Ga.: Maypop Books, 1987), 84.

26. "Old Joe and the Carpenter," reprinted with permission from *Thirty-Three Multi-Cultural Tales to Tell,* by Pleasant deSpain (Little Rock: August House Publishing, 1993), 13–14. This is a traditional tale from the southern United States that the author has adapted as his signature story. He says that the first recorded version is found in "A Job of Work," *North Carolina Folklore,* by Manly Wade Wellman, vol. 111, no. 1 (July 1955).

27. " The Sword of Wood," retold by Elisa Davy Pearmain. Published versions can be found in the following publications: *Elijah's Violin and Other Jewish Fairy Tales,* by Howard Schwartz (New York: Harper & Row, 1983), 89; *Folktales of Israel,* ed. Dov Noy (Chicago: University of Chicago Press, 1963), 73–75; *Gates to the Old City,* by Raphel Patai (Northvale, N.J.: Jason Aronson, 1980); and *The Classic Tales: 4000 Years of Jewish Lore,* by Ellen Franjel (Northvale, N.J.: Jason Aronson, 1989). I first heard this story from storyteller Doug Lipman. His version can be found in *Best Loved Stories Told at the National Storytelling Festival,* by the National Association for the Preservation and Perpetuation of Storytelling (Jonesborough, Tenn.: National Storytelling Press, 1991), 206–9, and on his audiotape *Milk from the Bull's Horn* (1986), published by Yellow Moon Press, Somerville, Mass. 1-800-497-4385.

28. "Water Not Wine," retold by Elisa Davy Pearmain. Two written versions include "The Feast," collected from the Bamum tribe, Cameroon, Africa, by H. Courlander, in *The King's Drum* (New York: Harcourt, Brace & World, 1962), 56–57, and "Ten Jugs of Wine," in *Sweet and Sour: Tales from China,* by Carol Kendall and Yoa-wen Li (New York: Clarion Books, 1979), 18–20.

29. "The Father, the Son, and the Donkey," retold by Elisa Davy Pearmain. Variants of this tale can be found from many countries, including: *Cambodian Folk Stories from the Gatiloke,* retold by Muriel Paskin Carrison from a translation by the Venerable Kong Chhean (Rutland, Vt.: Charles E. Tuttle Co., 1987), 102–6, and *Aesop's Fables,* translated by V. S. Vernon Jones (New York: Avenel Books, 1912), 136–38. It is also

attributed to Nasrudin and his son in *Tales of the Hodja,* by Charles Downing (New York: Henry Z. Walck, 1965), 21.

30. I heard "The Tree of Sorrows" from a friend's Jewish mother many years ago. I found a written version called "The Pekl Story," by Helen Mintz, in *Chosen Tales,* edited by Peninah Schram (Northvale, N.J.: Jason Aronson, 1995), 222–25, and another in *If You Meet the Buddha on the Road, Kill Him,* by Sheldon B. Kopp (New York: Bantam Books, 1972), 17. The *pekl* is the bag that the people put their troubles in. There is a story with a related motif in Margaret Geras's book The *Market of Miseries* (New York: Alfred A. Knopf, 1990), 66–76, in which a woman is allowed to shop for a different life and again chooses her own.

31. "Love Dogs," by Jelaluddin Rumi, from *The Essential Rumi,* by Coleman Barks (San Francisco: Harper SanFrancisco, 1995), 155–56. Used with the kind permission of Coleman Barks, poet and translator.

32. "The Torn Cloak," from Thomas Merton, *The Wisdom of the Desert.* Copyright 1960 The Abbey of Gethsemani, Inc., p. 40. Reprinted with permission of New Directions Publishing Corporation, New York. "Sin," adapted from *One Minute Wisdom,* by Anthony de Mello, S.J., p. 116. Copyright © (1985) by Anthony de Mello, S. J. Used by permission of Doubleday, a division of Bantam Doubleday Dell Publishing Group, Inc.

33. "Descent into the Maelstrom," retold in shortened and adapted form by Elisa Davy Pearmain from "A Descent into the Maelstrom," in *The Complete Stories and Poems of Edgar Allan Poe,* with permission from Doubleday & Co., Inc. (1996), Garden City, N.Y. It is well worth reading the original full-length version.

34. "The Difference between Heaven and Hell," retold by Elisa Davy Pearmain. Versions of this can be found in *Tales from Old China,* by Isabelle Chang (New York: Random House, 1948), 47–49, and *Peace Tales,* by Margaret Read MacDonald (Hamden, Conn.: Linnet Books, The Shoe String Press, 1992), 72. John Porcino has a lovely variant called "The Farmer and the Angel," which may come from a Christian adaptation in which, instead of being hampered by long chopsticks, the people's arms cannot bend. Found in *Spinning Tales, Weaving Hope,* edited by Ed Brody et al. (Philadelphia: New Society Publishers, 1992), 113–14.

35. "Only a Visitor," retold by Elisa Davy Pearmain. I heard this story from Jack Kornfield, who gave me permission to use it here. Written sources can be found in *The Song of the Bird,* by Anthony de Mello (New York: Doubleday, 1979), 137, and *Stories of the Spirit, Stories of the Heart,* by Jack Goldstein and Jack Kornfield (New York: HarperCollins, 1991), 347. For another story on the transitory nature of our time on earth, see "The Caravanserai," in *The Way of the Sufi,* by Idries Shah (London: Octagon Press, 1980), 238.

36. " The Messiah Is among Us," retold by Elisa Davy Pearmain. This story is thought to have Hasidic origins. I do not believe that I have traced it to its roots. Written versions include "The Rabbi's Gift," by Francis Dorff, in *New Catholic World* 222 (March–April 1979), 53, and in *Stories of the Spirit, Stories of the Heart,* by Christina Feldman and Jack Kornfield (New York: HarperCollins, 1991), 30–32.

37. "Survival," from *One Minute Wisdom,* by Anthony de Mello, S.J., p. 43.

Variants of this story include a Sufi version in which the student is given salted fish and no water. He thirsts all night for water and is told that he must thirst the same way for Allah. Source: *Wisdom of a Sufi Master, al-Jerrahi,* or *The Spirituality of Imperfection,* by Ernest Kurtz and Katherine Ketchem (New York: Bantam Books, 1992).

38. "The Wisdom of Allah," retold by Elisa Davy Pearmain. There are many versions of this tale. In some it is an eggplant and in others a watermelon that Nasrudin is pondering. I found versions in the following sources: *Tales of the Hodja,* by Charles Downing (New York: Henry Walck, 1965), 54; *Watermelons, Walnuts, and the Wisdom of Allah and Other Tales of the Hoca,* by Barbara Walker (New York: Parents Magazine Press, 1967); *Once the Hodja,* by Alice Geer Kelsey (New York: David McKay Co., 1943), 79–85; and *The Tales of Nasreddin Hodja Story Cards,* by Raymond C. Clark (Brattleboro, Vt.: Pro Lingua Associates, 1991).

39. "Blind Man Praying at the Wall," retold with permission from *Living Each Day,* by Rabbi Abraham Twerski, from The ArtScroll Series (Brooklyn, N.Y.: Mesorah Publications, 1988), 70. "I Am Prayer," retold from *Tales of the Hasidim: The Early Masters/The Later Masters,* by Martin Buber, translated by Olga Marx. Copyright 1947, 1948, Copyright renewed 1975 by Schocken Books, Inc., p. 252. Reprinted by permission of Schocken Books, distributed by Pantheon Books, a division of Random House, Inc.

40. "The Wild Strawberry," retold by Elisa Davy Pearmain. Written versions include *Zen Flesh, Zen Bones,* by Paul Reps (Rutland, Vt.: Charles E. Tuttle, 1957), 38–39; *Zen Buddhism* (Mount Vernon, N.Y.: Peter Pauper Press, 1959), 61; *One Hand Clapping: Zen Stories for All Ages,* by Rafe Martin (New York: Rizzoli International Publications, 1995), 8; and *Wisdom Tales from around the World,* by Heather Forest (Little Rock: August House Publishers, 1997), 40.

41. "The Trial of God," adapted by Elisa Davy Pearmain from a play, *The Trial of God,* by Elie Wiesel (New York: Random House, 1979), who witnessed one such trial in one of the concentration camps where he was held as a boy during World War II. This story was first told to me by our student minister, Susanne Skubik, who heard it in a lecture at Harvard Divinity School. I have borrowed from Susanne's adaptation. With generous permission from the author, Elie Wiesel, and Random House, N.Y.

42. "The King and His Falcon," retold by Elisa Davy Pearmain. There are many versions of this tale found in Asia and Europe. See "The Loyal Mongoose," in *The Panchatantra,* translated by Arthur W. Ryder (Chicago: University of Chicago Press, 1956), 432–34; *Fables and Fairy Tales,* by Leo Tolstoy (New York: Signet Books, 1962), 24; and *The Book of Virtues,* by William Bennett (New York: Simon & Schuster, 1993), 37–39. There is a fabulous retelling of this tale in "The Story That Saved a Life," by Kim R. Stafford, in which the author is literally saved from poisoning by recalling this story heard in childhood. Source: *Stories Lives Tell,* by C. Witherell and N. Noddings (New York: Teachers College Press, 1991), 23–25.

43. "A Drop of Honey," retold by Elisa Davy Pearmain. Written variants on this motif include *A Kingdom Lost for a Drop of Honey and Other Burmese Folktales,* by

Maung Htin Aung and Helen G. Trager (New York: Parents Magazine Press, 1968), 29–30; "Not Our Problem," retold by Margaret Read MacDonald in *Peace Tales* (Hamden, Conn.: Linnet Books/Shoe String Press, 1992), 18–20; *Burmese and Thai Fairy Tales*, by Eleanor Brockett (Chicago: Follett, 1965), 150–52; and *Tales from Thailand*, by Marian Davies Toth (Rutland, Vt.: Charles E. Tuttle Co., 1971), 41–48. The latter two versions stress controlling one's temper rather than taking responsibility. Thanks to Margaret Read MacDonald for introducing this one to the storytelling community.

44. "The Lost Key," retold by Elisa Davy Pearmain. This is one of the most often repeated of the Nasrudin stories. Find it in the following collections: *Tales of the Hodja*, by Charles Downing (New York: Henry Z. Walck, 1965), 71, and *The Exploits of the Incomparable Mulla Nasrudin*, by Idries Shah (New York: Simon & Schuster, 1966), 24.

45. "The Three Questions," retold by Elisa Davy Pearmain. Written versions of this story can be found in *Fables and Fairy Tales*, by Leo Tolstoy (New York: Signet Classics, The New American Library, 1962), 82–88; and *One Hand Clapping: Zen Stories for All Ages*, by Rafe Martin (New York: Rizzoli International Publications, 1995), 18.

46. I first heard "The Wounded Healer," which comes originally from the Talmud, from Rev. Roger Paine. From "Before the Gates of Rome," in *A Jewish Reader: In Time and Eternity*, ed. Nahum N. Glatzer, trans. Olga Mark Perlzweig. Copyright 1946 and renewed 1974 by Schocken Books, Inc. Copyright © 1961 by Schocken Books, Inc. Reprinted by permission of Schocken Books, distributed by Pantheon Books, a division of Random House, Inc.

47. "Feathers," retold by Elisa Davy Pearmain. This story is widely told in the storytelling community. Written versions include "The Gossip," by Marcia Lane, in *Spinning Tales, Weaving Hope*, edited by Ed Brody et al. (Philadelphia: New Society Publishers, 1992), 143, and *Wisdom Tales from around the World*, by Heather Forest (Little Rock: August House Publishers, 1996), 67–69. There is an interesting kids' adaptation called "The Gossipy Child," in *Easy to Tell Stories for Young Children*, by Annette Harrison (Jonesborough, Tenn.: National Storytelling Press, 1992), 65–68.

48. "The Bag of Gold," reprinted with slight adaptation by permission of Riverhead Books, a division of The Putnam Group, from *Kitchen Table Wisdom* by Rachel Naomi Remen (CITY: Riverhead Books, 1996). Copyright © 1996 by Rachel Naomi Remen, M.D. I was unable to find a traditional written source for this Hindu legend. The story was first brought to my attention by my student Brigid Surber. Dr. Remen heard it from one of her patients.

49. "The Legend of the Mistletoe," by Diane Edgecomb. © 1997. All rights reserved; Wilderwalks Productions, PO Box 300016, Boston, MA 02130; www.livingmyth.com; dedge@livingmyth.com; (617) 522-4335. This story is based upon a Scandinavian legend. The quote in the follow-up section is from the book *The Spirituality of Imperfection*, by Ernest Kurtz and Katherine Ketchem (New York: Bantam Books, 1992), 223.

50. "Jesus' Cloak," from the Gospels of Mark 5:25-34 and Luke 8:43-48, New Revised Standard Version, © 1989 by the Division of Christian Education of the National Council of the Churches of Christ in the U.S.A. Thanks to Rev. Roger Paine for introducing me to this story.

51. "You're Still Carrying Her," retold by Elisa Davy Pearmain. This story is widely told in the storytelling community. Some written sources are found in *The Song of the Bird*, by Anthony de Mello (New York: Doubleday, 1984), 108, and the "Muddy Road" in *Zen Flesh, Zen Bones*, by Paul Reps (Rutland, Vt.: Charles E. Tuttle, 1947). A different version in which a monk carries a leper across the stream and midstream she transforms into a god, can be found in *Stories of the Spirit, Stories of the Heart*, by Christina Feldman and Jack Kornfield (New York: HarperCollins, 1991), 229.

52. "The Question," adapted from *Tales of the Hasidim: The Early Masters/The Later Masters*, by Martin Buber, translated by Olga Marx. Copyright 1947, 1948, copyright renewed 1975 by Schocken Books, Inc., p. 251. Reprinted by permission of Schocken Books, distributed by Pantheon Books, a division of Random House, Inc. First told to me by storyteller Doug Lipman. See the resources section for more information about Doug.

RESOURCES ON SPIRITUALITY
AND STORYTELLING

⌒

BOOKS ON MEDITATION

Herbert Benson, M.D., *The Relaxation Response* (New York: William Morrow &
Co., 1975).

Joan Borysenko, *Mending the Mind, Minding the Body* (New York: Bantam
Books, 1988). See her many other books and tapes as well.

Ram Dass, *Journey of Awakening: A Meditator's Guidebook* (New York: Bantam
Books, 1978).

Joseph Goldstein and Jack Kornfield, *The Heart of the Enlightened* (Boston:
Shambhala Books, 1987).

Jon Kabat-Zinn, *Mindfulness Meditation* (New York: Simon & Schuster, 1995).

Lawrence LeShan, *How to Meditate: A Guide to Self-Discovery* (Boston: Little,
Brown & Co., 1974).

Stephen Levine, *A Gradual Awakening* (New York: Doubleday, 1979).

Thích Nhât Hanh, *The Miracle of Mindfulness: A Manual of Meditation*
(Boston: Beacon Press, 1987).

STORYTELLING RESOURCES AND ORGANIZATIONS

The National Storytelling Association, Jonesborough, Tenn. 1-800-525-4514. A
bimonthly magazine, annual festival and conference, clearinghouse for storytelling-related activities nationwide. Call for their free catalog of storytelling resources and for information about groups and events in your area.

Yellow Moon Press, Somerville, Mass. 1-800-497-4385. Call for their free catalog of storytelling resources.

Contact Storytell at storytell-request@venus.twu.edu to join this free Internet
listserv group. Take part in lively discussions on many aspects of storytelling. Seek help in finding stories or storytelling-related information from
others. To send messages the address is storytell@venus.twu.edu. Warning:
You will receive up to 50 messages a day!

Storyteller Doug Lipman's Hasidic Stories Website. Read new Hasidic stories
each month and articles about them, and find out about Doug's many
books and tapes at www.hasidic@storypower.com.

To find out more about the author's storytelling program and workshops, go to
her Web site at www.storynet.org.

INDEX OF THEMES

(I n d e x e d   b y   s t o r y   n u m b e r .)

135